My own understanding is the sole treasure I possess, and the greatest. Though infinitely small and fragile in comparison with the powers of darkness, it is still a light, my only light.

Carl G. Jung
Memories, Dreams, Reflections

The Author

Natalie Rogers, M.A., is co-founder and Creative Director of The Person Centered Expressive Therapy Institute in Santa Rosa, California. She is trained in client-centered therapy, movement, art therapy and feminist theory. In 1975 she initiated with her father, Carl Rogers, residential workshops in "The Person Centered Approach."

As an international facilitator she has led groups focusing on women's issues and workshops on "Fostering Creativity" in Latin America, Europe, Japan and the Soviet Union.

Natalie has taught at the California Institute of Transpersonal Psychology, The University of San Francisco and John F. Kennedy University.

As of this second edition of Emerging Woman (1989) two of her daughters and three grandchildren live in Northern California. Her oldest daughter and grandson live in Massachusetts.

EMERGING WOMAN

A Decade of
Midlife Transitions

Natalie Rogers

PCCS BOOKS
Manchester

First published by Personal Press, Santa Rosa, California in 1980

Reprinted in 1995 by
PCCS BOOKS
Paragon House
48 Seymour Grove
Old Trafford
Manchester
M16 OLN

Emerging Woman - A Decade of Midlife Transitions

ISBN 1 898059 11 X

Cover drawing and artwork throughout the book by Natalie Rogers
Printed by Printoff Graphic Arts Ltd, Nelson, Lancs. 01282 61222

CONTENTS

CONTENTS

INTRODUCTION
to First Edition, 1980 —

This book is written to give women courage and support to be full persons in our society; and to point out that what is personal is political. That is, what we choose to think and do as individuals has impact on our society as a whole.

It is also written to give sanction to men and women to be honest and open about their struggles. Communication begins by revealing oneself. I have revealed much of myself in the hope that it will stimulate new thought and action; new channels to reach out to each other.

I also wish to alert people that they can be in charge of their own transitions; we know that change is here to stay; we need to understand how to nurture ourselves through the cycles of endings and beginnings—to understand something of the process involved.

The special quality of this book is that it is like a human being, it has been in process and constantly changes. The changes show. The first chapter is the me that existed in 1970 and the last chapters, "Opening" and "The Impact of Women," is the me that exists now. The years 1970-1980 have been an important, frustrating, exciting, discovering decade—my mid-years between age forty and fifty.

Although I share my personal journey, it is more than that: I am also reflecting on the learnings and concepts I gain as I look at my transitions. I am learning from my own life experiences, not to tell you "how to do it," but with an understanding that what is deeply personal is universal.

At age forty, as the first chapter germinated, I was struggling and fighting for "The Right To Be Me!" I looked at what was expected of me as a girl-child and how that affected the role I took on as a married woman. Of the nineteen years of married life—twelve of them being warm, loving, and exciting—I focus on episodes which demeaned, angered, and intimidated me; and describe the internal process by which I pulled myself out. I discovered the personal meaning of what it is like to live in a male-dominated society.

"Uprooting and Rerooting," Chapter Two, describes my transition in moving from my home of twenty-four years on the

7

East Coast to California. Through the fears and craziness that happen with such a major shift, I analyze my decision-making process, my way of building a bridge to the new environment, the pain of saying farewell and letting go of the past, the disorientation and feelings of being in limbo in my new location, and some ways that I put down roots. I ask myself a major question: "Who am I when I am not depending on anyone? And when no one is depending on me?" I found some helpful strategies in times of transition.

The "Solo" chapter was prompted when I realized I had pulled myself out of a marriage in which I was dying emotionally, but I had not chosen to be *alone.* In writing this section I discovered the difference, for me, beween being alone and being lonely—they are not the same. I tested myself on a three-day solo in the desert. I discovered that if I have an identity— an inner core or center—then times of being alone become times of creativity and self expression or of peaceful meditation.

Writing on "Love, Loving, and Lovers" was a way of gleaning the learnings from many surprising and difficult situations. When I sorted out the vignettes, I realized my attitudes towards relationships had changed a great deal in five or six years of trial and error. What had at first been a search for another "permanent" partner and father for my children turned into looking for a relationship in which I could be both independent and *inter*-dependent; where I could have equal power and control in a relationship while being tender, loving, and sexual. The need for permanence and monogamy had shifted to a need for a relationship where I could be fully myself (which includes being *equal*). One theme in this chapter is my constant search for better ways to relate with partners; the other is the politics of the partner relationship. "What I allow to exist in my heart and in my bedroom will exist in the larger society."

The chapter, "Opening," pulls together the experiences I have had which *change the lens* from which I view the world. I have found this inward journey at least as important as my activist, outreaching path. "As I near fifty, my transition in life seems to be the journey in search of my inner truth; the integration of the polarities—the masculine and feminine, the yin and yang—or the opposing forces within."

In the final chapter, I needed to explore my attitudes and experiences with women. As I paced the floor trying to separate out the puzzle pieces—which is my mother and which is me—I discovered new aspects of myself. My own values and priorities crystallized. In understanding that my mother did what she wanted in her life, as best she could, I came face to face with the question: "What is it I want for myself? Stop asking *her* to be what I want for *me!*"

As I thought about my women friends of the last ten years, I realized they had been the source and supporters of this book. It is a painfully slow process—self-discovery through writing. It also stirs deep the kettle of emotions. Arduous as it is, however, it is easier than sharing that writing with the public. So encouragement and interest from these women has been my sustenance.

This book, including the pictures from my photo album and my personal art journal, is meant to be an *experience*. I hope it is a meaningful one for you.

INTRODUCTION
to Second Edition

Dear Readers:

It seems like a miracle to me that this book, which first started as a form of self-understanding and personal awareness, is now in its second edition. It has been eight years since I first self-published this book. Not only have 10,000 copies sold in the United States, but *Emerging Woman* is now published in French (Canada), German, Portuguese (Brazil), Italian and Japanese. It is also fully translated into Spanish awaiting some publisher to take it. The amazing part is that women and men have passed this book on to friends, colleagues, lovers, husbands, wives and even into the hands of people in other lands. I have received correspondence from many countries as well as all parts of the U.S. saying "you have told my story, it gives me courage, thanks." Here are a few of the quotes that helped me realize that in sharing my personal journey I have contributed to the lives of others:

> "All I can say is, 'WOW' and I wish I had read it when I was first divorced."

> "Your book inspires me to fulfill my dreams."

> "I think I understand now, the trauma my ex-wife went through before we finally divorced and I could get a feel for your ex-husband's surprise and anger for I was also brought up to buy those macho roles."

> "Your beautifully written truth is happening to me within the marriage. . . This book affirms Life."

> And one man wrote, "This is rocking my foundations."

Emerging Woman was written between 1975 and 1980. I was 51 when the book was completed. Now, I am 60. It would take another 10 chapters to follow up on all of the personal/political issues in this book, but for now I wish to emphasize the professional path which has integrated my life.

My self healing came as I wrote this book. It is the transformative power of creative expression—whether it is through the written word, visual art, movement or music—that is my life focus, now.

In 1984 I founded, with my daughter Frances Fuchs, the Person Centered Expressive Therapy Institute, an international training program dedicated to exploring the creative process to enhance self-esteem and self-empowerment. The program is a three generational living extension of the work of my father, Carl Rogers. We are a cross-cultural network of people exploring the creative process to enrich lives, to pursue solutions for peace and to develop spiritual connection.

My life and work is focused on the creative process. I have the pleasure of seeing people come to full bloom as they explore and experiment in the safe, lively learning environments we create. Artists, writers, musicians, business people and professionals in the mental health field come to re-discover their innate creativity.

I believe that each of us has within us both the longing and the ability to be creative. During childhood, however, a lid is put on that creative source because teachers, parents and friends tell us such things as:"You are clumsy and shouldn't dance,"or "That piece of art work deserves a C," or "This is the way you SHOULD play this piano piece." So, we lose our self-confidence and enjoyment of what is natural and spontaneous. We become self conscious in movement or in using paints or clay to express ourselves. Some people even become blocked in their ability to write.

I also believe that our emotions are a source for creativity. Feelings of fear, love, rage, or grief can be channeled into expressive modes such as movement, art, or poetry. (The pictures in this book and on the cover are testimony to such expression). As we release these feelings we gain a sense of our own identity and as we look at how others have expressed themselves we begin to appreciate the human qualities of all people. The creative process is like freedom, once you've tasted it you cannot do without it. It connects us across cultures as non-verbal communication carrying the inner truths beyond political boundaries.

Recently I've had the good fortune of being able to teach/facilitate such groups in creativity in many countries of Europe, Latin America, Japan and the Soviet Union. My next book will combine this personal journey of self-discovery, spiritual development and theoretical learnings from these many experiences. The richness of my personal life has grown in joining with others to foster creativity.

If you are interested in this work, I hope you'll write to me at: The Person Centered Expressive Therapy Institute, P.O. Box 6518, Santa Rosa, CA 95406, U.S.A.

Natalie Rogers
March, 1989

1
The Right to Be Me! Confronting Sex Role Expectations

Part One

Expectations in Childhood and Marriage

I have spent some time trying to discover how I came to be the woman I am. How much of what I am was set by cultural role expectations? What, in my childhood, adolescence, and adult life was prescribed for me? How much freedom do I have to *choose* my role? What is it I want? In order to understand the role expectations placed on me, I have looked for those people and incidents which have influenced my attitudes toward myself.

Metaphors of Childhood

As I look back on my girlhood, I see myself in a sailboat. It is a small, tubby boat my father had built in our garage. Mother made the sails—their division of labor. We were proud of the stability of the "Snark" even though it was not the sleek racing boat that others sailed on the lake.

"Come on, Nat, want to join me for a sail?" My brother takes the initiative. "See if you can put up the jib, I'll rig the mainsail. You can hold the tiller while I shove off .... Okay, good girl, get to the jib and pull the sheets in. The jib will pull us round . . . . There we go, swell—we can relax now. When I get us away from this tricky shore wind I'll let you take the tiller."

As the wind fills the mainsail and I pull tight the jib to keep it from luffing, I feel proud. I hope I'm doing it right. As we heel in the wind I let it out a little; and, looking to the captain, I ask, "Is this okay?"

"Well, you could let it out a little further," comes the knowledgeable reply. I tidy the boat, coiling the ropes, looping the end through the coil, and hanging it neatly on the cleat. As we gain full speed, the wind strokes my face and excitement wells inside me. I look at my brother with question in my eyes, "Now?"

"Okay, you can take the tiller, but take it easy, the gusts come up suddenly."

As we switch places the boat levels off, I pull in the mainsail, hold the tiller tight, and heel us until the deck is cutting the lake.

"You've got it too tight! We'll go faster if you let it out," comes the advice.

I know this is true, but I enjoy the risky feeling of balancing on the edge. I slice the water, bracing my feet against the cockpit, leaning hard against the rope. A storm cloud appears. My brother announces that he is taking us in. I relinquish my seat feeling secure in his presence.

The memory of sailing in the boat with my father and brother is a simple, joyful recollection. Being the crew for one or two men skippers while Mom was on the shore making lunch has become a significant metaphor in my development as a female. I was proud to be a good crew: I knew how to keep the boat shipshape to the requirements of the captains. As crew, I was pleasing the men in my life, getting their praise for doing what was expected of me. It was exciting to me to be a part of their action. I didn't have to take command of the boat—I liked that feeling of being protected from the full responsibility, yet being part of the excitement. I used to think, "Too bad for you, Mom, you're not out here with the adventure of making the boat heel, or of racing toward home before the squall comes up." I must have felt proud to be included with the men and somewhat disdainful of the woman left on shore, yet glad that she was there with the warm soup when we got back.

It doesn't take an analyst to see that I was being well trained for my role as a woman. I wanted to please the man I loved, to take part in their more exciting world, to take the tiller only on occasion (to take responsibility for the direction of others only occasionally), and with their approval and guidance. Mother's life was necessary and appreciated—but not as exciting. There was, and still is, an element in me that says, "I'll be more adventurous than you." Though I was appreciated, loved, and included, the expectation seemed to be that I would not be capable of being captain of a ship. I would ask for a turn at the tiller with full knowledge that I could only be second best. They (the men) had the *real* understanding of how things worked.

As a girl, I was being subtly trained to believe:

Men take the major responsibility for leadership and direction in life. They are to have control.

Women are to be helpers toward the destination that men choose. A good helper is pleasing, serving, accommodating.

Men have the real knowledge and understanding; women ask them for the truth.

Women get their "goodies" (self-esteem) by being praised and adored for being all of the above!

These were all an unspoken part of my growing up, and I never thought to question this role. It is only recently, in the process of writing these pages and leading women's groups, that I have come to realize what such training did to limit the scope of my personal horizons.

I am now aware that the seeds of some of my present

anger started germinating in childhood, as my parents and brother acted out the roles society demanded of them.

Looking at a favorite snapshot of me and my older brother, I see us standing on the back porch—he with his arm protectively around my shoulders. The expression on my face says I am enjoying cuddling under his wing. What a comforting role, this! And to this day, when a man puts his arm around me with the "I'll take care of you" stance, I yield to that longing. But I *now* know I can allow myself to be temporarily protected as long as it is not my role in *life*.

As a model for being a wife and mother, my mother set very high standards. She was nurturing and supportive, always there to do things for us, feed us, and take care of us. She cooked, cleaned, did the laundry, took care of our needs for love, discipline, schooling, and play. My father worked long hours in a clinic for disturbed children and wrote at night. She was taking care to see that he had the time to do his important work and would not need to be bothered with the mundane things in life. Although she had interests of her own, the message from mother was that "Children and husband come first, my own needs come last." We prospered under this in many ways, but at what cost to her? This model played some havoc with me. When it came to my own marriage, I took on that same model without questioning whether it was right for me.

The words "career woman" were pejorative in our home. They meant being cold, unfeminine, unmotherly, competitive, and aggressive. It was a wife's role to be emotionally supportive, to do everything possible to promote her husband's ideas and profession. Of course, in those days, I never consciously thought about what my parents were to each other or what impressions it left on me. I saw them peacefully discussing issues. I saw them caring and touching each other. I observed the division of labor and the feeling of who was dealing with the "world" and who was taking care of "home." Later I acted on what I had learned without being aware of it.

Marriage: Collusion of Two Members for the Benefit of One

The night before my wedding, like the picture of the sailboat, is a clear memory:

I can't sleep, naturally. I'm too excited. It's hard to believe tomorrow is the day I've dreamed of for so long. Marriage, to the one I will always love—my heart feels large, warm, and tender.

Amazing I have no doubts or fears. Some brides do, I know. I just want to give and be loved and share our lives. I wonder, wonder what our life will be like now that we are sealing it forever? Sounds delicious. I'm so happy I could burst!

I remember the choices I *thought* I had when I graduated from college. "If I don't find a man to marry I'll go on to graduate school to become a psychologist." It seemed like a very lonely possible second choice. It never occurred to me I could do both. Nor did anyone expect me to do both.

In retrospect, what I did to myself and how my husband colluded with me in the state of matrimony is incredible. I wrote to him, before marriage, that I thought he was better at most things than I, and that I looked forward to "living my life for him." When I read this "love" letter twenty years later, I set a match to it instantly. As I did so, I realized that I had been asking him to be the graduate student, the psychologist, the political activist, the thinker, and doer, when that is what I wanted for myself. I *married* one instead of *becoming* one.

The fact that I was at least as good as my husband-to-be in all areas—in human relations, in intellectual ability, in the "how to fix it" department, in life experience of being independent and responsible for myself—was somehow forgotten as I entered into a commitment to be a wife. To this day, I don't know whether my feelings of self-worth were really that low or whether I was responding to the powerful pressures of what a good wife is supposed to be. Apparently, being second best was one of my definitions of love.

I had applied to graduate school at Harvard (where he had already been accepted). I was told I wouldn't be accepted unless I was a full-time student. In this same letter to my fiancé, I wrote, "It will take at least half-time to take care of you." This was said without malice or resentment. It was what I expected of myself. The concept that we might share equally in educational opportunities and in taking care of each other never occurred to either of us. Instead, I edited, typed, helped organize his papers, occasionally went with him to classes to take his notes, or to the library to assist him in research. He was proud of all that I did, giving me praise—apparently I enjoyed and needed this approval. It kept me doing the second-class work throughout our marriage. I don't even remember wondering why I wasn't going to classes and writing papers for myself. No one else asked why either.

Why should a man question what this role does to a woman? His ego and his work benefit greatly from this system. I was quite content with my role. I seemed to go to any length to get praise and approval. It was making a gourmet casserole, or the most original hors d'oeuvre, or running an efficient and tasteful house—that kept me going. Not that there is anything inherently wrong with any of those achievements. But what was happening to my *brain?* Except for the times that I was helping him think through the data for his books, or the decisions he had to make, or how to teach his class, I was not developing my own ability to think. I was hiding behind his ideas. He was using my thoughts in his work (without giving me credit).

I seldom said, "This is my opinion," or "These are the dilemmas in the world as I view them." My identity as a thinking person, capable of sifting information, analyzing and coming to conclusions, was given over to him. I believe was acting out what was expected of me by my family, my husband, and society, without questioning any of it.

And yet, what a contrast to the person I had started

to become before my marriage. In college I was quite a strong, independent-thinking young woman. At a woman's college I was turned on by new ideas, by testing my own intelligence. Delving into philosophy, religion, and literature, I questioned my own beliefs, or lack of them, searching for my place in the universe. (In a coed high school I had known well the need to act less intelligent than I was in order to be attractive to the boys.) Now I thrived on the personal attention of the professors—women and men—who wanted to hear about my philosophical struggles. I was valued for my ability to think and enjoyed the intellectual sparring with adults; and, since there were no men in the classes, I did not hold myself back intellectually. When I married, apparently I took off my thinking cap.

One part of the marriage myth that did not disappoint me was motherhood. I truly enjoyed being a mother and put a lot of my creative energy and intelligence into being with my children. I treasured being with my daughters while they were young. I experienced them as important persons from the day they responded to my love with a smile—and that was the day they were born! (No doctor will ever convince me those smiles were due to "gas bubbles.")

Playing with my children was fun. For hours I'd sit on the floor building blocks, crayoning, watching, encouraging, and chatting while they discovered how to hammer down the peg or build a tower. Their discoveries were exciting to me.

When I pushed Janet in the stroller to the park, I was happy to be alone with her. Some mothers sat together on a bench more interested in each other than their kids—which puzzled me.

When the girls were older, I created Sunday art-time where materials and possible projects with paint, collage, and clay were available to all of us at the kitchen table. As a family we enjoyed our playtimes together.

However, I resented having to be the sole disciplinarian of the family, and this was the one issue in our marriage that I assertively fought about. As bedtime approached, father and daughters would be happily engaged in story telling. Fine!

Except that usually there was no ending to it unless I put my foot down. It was like having a fourth child—since I had to convince him to close the books or end the tale, as well. My request for shared responsibility for the disciplining was not heard. In the various parent groups I have run, this is one of the biggest complaints on the part of mothers: not being able to get fathers to share in the necessary task of setting appropriate limits for the children and consistently following them through. My husband preferred the role of playmate to the kids when they were young, rather than accept his share of the disciplining. I felt like the ogre.

If I were to relive my married life, I would still choose to spend most of my time, for those twelve to fifteen years, being a mother. It is one of the most enjoyable careers I can imagine. But I would also have a different attitude about my rights to time off and sharing of household responsibilities. I would not feel guilty when I took time for myself to read, write, study, or be with others.

By a subtle process which many women will recognize, I began to lose my identity in the marriage. His friends and colleagues became my friends. His career became my motivation. I protected and promoted his time and space to work. The telephone rang constantly—for him. Our system was that I would answer it, screen the call as to its immediate importance, and interrupt his writing or thinking only if absolutely necessary. I was a competent receptionist—but who protected any time for me?

Those were the days I would be introduced as Mrs. ———. The first question asked me was, "What does your husband do?" And I'd be discussing his involvements for hours. It occurred to me one week when he was out of town that I didn't really know who I was when he was gone. My identity was defined by his presence. Who was I and what did I believe in when he was away?

> He was torn about leaving me to go on this speaking tour. Having him gone for a week is a totally new experience. Is it possible that except for my three trips to the hospital to give birth, we have not been apart one night in eight years? I think

it is true. I have such mixed feelings—I'm glad to have a few evenings to myself after the kids are in bed, and yet I don't feel I am all here. Part of me walked out the door and got in that taxi.

Having S. here alone for supper was a nice experience. She didn't seem to think anything was strange, but as we sat eating leftover pot roast (the kids had eaten) and talking about life—her thoughts and mine—I realized I didn't *have* many thoughts of my own. Or do I? I'm just not used to saying them. I'm not sure my opinions or knowledge have validity anymore. I feel I depend on my husband's interpretation or answers for everything (outside of the house and children). S. seemed interested in my opinions—she certainly has hers!

This gives me some new insights. I need to do something about me. If I don't talk about him and his work, or my kids and their life, what *do* I talk about? More importantly, what do I think about if I'm not thinking of them?

Once I recognized how symbiotic we were, it became important to me to re-establish my own areas of interest. I decided to go back to school in the field of psychology. The encouragement of Abe Maslow helped me gain courage to become a student. (I already felt I was too old and stale to compete at age thirty.) I had also gained support from my father over the years to publish my psychological writing ("Play Therapy at Home," 1957: *Merrill-Palmer Quarterly*, Winter).[1] Today, as I counsel women, I often hear their sense of isolation and lack of self-worth as they toy with the idea of further education. I know how important supportive individuals can be at that time.

I had adopted the notion that a man's work is always more important than a woman's. Therefore, when I started graduate school, I took one course a semester, feeling somewhat guilty as I rushed off to school while my husband babysat. He made me feel this was something he was "giving" me, for which I should be grateful. It didn't occur to me (or to him) that I was entitled to further education. Neither of us imagined

[1]Also published in Clark Moustakas' book, *Psychotherapy With Children, The Living Relationship*. It appears in the chapter, "Parents as Therapists."

that my work was important as work, or that my ideas might contribute just as much to the world as his.

The ultimate in thinking "His work is more important than mine" was captured in a rather humorous event. I was nine months' pregnant and close to delivery. My husband, on leaving for work, reminded me what a very important day this was in his career. "Don't have the baby today," he said. A fetus doesn't seem to have the same accommodating personality as a wife, so I did have the baby that day. When I called to let him know his important day was going to be interrupted by me and our child, I apologized rather than acknowledged that my work of the day was *more* important than his.

When I look at our photo album I see pictures of a loving honeymoon in Europe with our tiny English car, hikes and picnics with the kids, birthday celebrations and travels. There is warmth in our faces, radiance and laughter in the children. Together. As many hours of as many days as possible, together. We shared our lives focusing on the world and the children. Bedtime stories, Saturday walks, family art projects on Sundays. Together we built a nest, a house out of which each of us could fly, only to return to its safety and warmth.

> My wings seem to be broken, or is it a cage I am in? Each time I go out for a test flight and come back, I awake the next day, my wings hurting. Am I so afraid to fly? Or is the male bird in this nest putting holes in my wings when I'm not aware of it? He says, "Go, I am proud to see you fly!" Yet the nest feels cold when I return. I ache.
>
> Is he aware that every time I test out an idea or opinion at the dinner table he either puts it down, pushes it aside, or talks on endlessly until I am lost in the fog? I lose my sense of self.
>
> Or does he realize that when I come home after class or writing my thesis that there is hostility in the air? Or pouting?

. . .and a year later:

What is wrong with me? Every day I drive to pick up Janet at the end of the MTA line as she comes home from high school. And every day I get on the highway and miss the exit! It seems dangerous that I can't keep my mind on the road. Then I turn around to go back to the exit and discover I've passed it again! Where was my mind? Why do I think of death all the time? Why? When I love my kids, I have a nice home, I have a husband who loves me (we never argue), I have security. Why am I in this awful funk?

Who Am I?

To the outside world the image of our marriage was of two handsome people doing exciting things. Inside, I was lonely and unhappy, and blamed it totally on myself. I would look at the trees silhouetted against the orange sky of the setting sun and say to myself, "I know that is an exquisite scene and in years past I would *feel* it. Now I am dead inside."

Women, I find, tend to blame the failure of marriage on themselves. As the carriers of the emotional condition of a relationship, they feel they are to blame if something goes wrong.

It is apparent to me now that I was unaware of my needs and feelings and had little ability to express my resentments or demand rights for myself.

Today, I can also see that part of my depression was caused by society's role expectation—my feelings of inadequacy were built into the system. This system we have created produces second-class citizenship for women and causes much pain.

My emotional pain found vent in constant fantasies of flight, of packing my bags and leaving without saying good-bye to anyone since *I* couldn't understand—to say nothing of trying to explain to the children I loved—why I felt I had to go. My other fantasy was the peace of total oblivion or nonexistence. This eventually worked its way into many specific fantasies of death, with all the attached guilt feelings for even thinking of leaving the people who loved me.

It was a bright sunny New England Sunday, but I could *feel* nothing. My husband and children were home. Life seemed normal, whatever that meant. There were no fights or hassles. Inside I was so empty and numb. I remember telling my husband and children that I was going to take the car for the day—to be alone. (An unusual event for me.) Without knowing where I was going or why, I started driving. I remember stopping as I went on a country road, not to *do* anything, just to turn around. Back to what? Away from what? I was confused, groggy, didn't know. I saw a Turnpike sign and followed it. Started West with no destination, no inkling if I would return. Tears rolled down my face as I was driving. It was as though the dam broke loose—I could barely see—yet there was no pain. My foot got heavy on the accelerator. I pushed it to ninety. "My God, why doesn't a cop stop me?" I thought. Part of me was hoping that someone would see me speeding and report me. Another part of me wanted to hit the railing on the next curve. Three hours went by without stopping—the tears kept flowing. As my foot got tired from pressing the accelerator, I exited on to a country road. I came to a halt in front of a pond with a marshy bottom and cat-tails. I sat for how long? An hour or two wondering if I could drive me and the car into the pond to an end. Wondering what was wrong with me, feeling blank.

As I began to experience my mortality, my choice—to end my life or to live—I finally felt the pain. I sobbed and sobbed. This time with feeling. Feeling of potential loss of my children and their potential loss of me. Love and guilt. Who would help me understand me? Who would care? Who would see beyond the reserved, collected, smooth exterior? Who would see beyond the pretty face and graceful body? My loneliness was profound. I felt alienated from myself, from the ones I loved, and the world. I felt completely vulnerable. If anyone ever knew what I had just been through, would they forgive me? Would I forgive myself? As I sat in the car staring at the muck of the pond which mirrored my internal state, I looked at my own death, and took the first step back to myself.

Finding some paper to scribble on, I wrote a note to a psychiatrist colleague: "Would you help me? I think I'm destroying our marriage." (Notice where I put the blame.)

When I returned home, I found my husband and

daughters having a quiet, creative Sunday with art materials—
something I had always initiated for the family. It was eerie to
see them carry on with my project, as though I were already
dead—as though at some level they knew what had happened
to me that day. I said to myself, "Yes, they could go on without
me. My husband would take on those duties and character-
istics which are mine, and life would continue in my absence."
It was sobering. Rather than have them ask me questions
about my day, I went to a movie. By morning, life had returned
to normal; or so we pretended.

That timid note to the psychiatrist was a muted scream. If
I had told the truth, I would have said, "I feel like I am being
swallowed up alive—there is nothing left of me, and I would
just as soon disappear into the mist as to be devoured by this
relationship."

It was a big step for me to say, "I'm hurting—I need
help." I knew people needed me, but I didn't know that I
needed people. With help, I began to work my way out of the
bottom of the well by finding my own strengths and voicing
some of my needs. What I needed was room to change, and
support in my experiments and learnings. I needed to be
myself instead of all those things *expected of me*. Eventually, I
went to a five-day workshop without my husband or children.
My mother encouraged me in taking this step. She thought it
would be an enriching experience for me, and offered to take
care of my children and husband in my absence. It was the
first time I had been on my own since my marriage thirteen
years earlier. I was amazed when people responded to me as a
warm, intelligent, caring human being with my own identity.
People were relating to *me*—not as wife, not as mother, but
just plain me. It was like coming out from under the deep
shade of a tree where others could only vaguely see me, into
the bright sunlight, where I stood in full view. Both the
warmth and the exposure seemed risky and exhilarating.

I think the process by which a woman loses her identity in
marriage is well expressed in an article by a *man*, Joel Roache,
in *Ms.* magazine. He took care of the home while his wife had

a turn at her career. He describes very clearly his initial joy in doing the job well. However as time went on, the demands of the job left no time for himself, and his transformation from a self-assured individual to an angry, unsympathetic second-class citizen was complete. He says, "I was getting my sense of fulfillment, of self-esteem, through *her*, while she was getting it through her work. I was a full-fledged house-husband."

Marriage in Crisis

During the next few years, our marriage was in "an identity crisis" as Margaret Mead defines it: "For years the wife, always alert and attentive to the immediate needs of her family for food and comfort, clothes and transportation, play and rest, seldom has thought of herself alone. Then one day she begins to look more carefully at...what it means to become a person with goals of one's own, as distinguished from a total commitment to homemaking. But such a crisis is not—or need not become—a catastrophe. It is also a signal that the partners are ready, if they can but find their way, for a new stage of living together. They are ready, if each is willing for the other to grow as a person, to broaden and deepen what they have to share."

We tried, during this period, to understand what each other's needs were. We had long talks, and went to our first marriage counselor. Unfortunately, she listened to my verbal husband delve into his childhood years while I sat in mute pain as the scenario of our relationship was re-enacted in her presence, without her recognizing my silent agony. Today, when I counsel couples, I am acutely aware of "equal time for each" and of the poignant non-verbal messages being sent. There I was, in the counselor's office, listening, as usual, while the talk show went on.

I made efforts to establish my new feelings of selfhood within the marriage relationship. I was certainly gaining a sense of myself outside of the relationship. But the ways my husband maintained control and created dependence were numerous. As I started to earn a couple of thousand dollars a year, I was excited by my new sense of self-worth; and I "asked" my husband if I might put the money in an account of my own to spend on special gifts from me to our family, such as family vacations. He said "No." In this instance, I am not sure whether my husband was blind to my need to feel good about my small earning power, or whether he wanted to maintain control of the family purse. Now I wonder, why did I *give away my power* by "asking?" I could have told him what I planned to do with the money. By training and role expectation, women frequently hand the power to men without realizing it.

At one point, I said I wanted to buy my own car—that is, to shop, evaluate, bargain, and make a decision. Distasteful though it was, I took it as a challenge. Somehow, at the last minute, my spouse went out and made the final choice, negotiated the final deal, and proudly brought the car home to me. This took away my sense of power and exemplified his inability to understand my need to relearn the self-sufficiency I had when I was twenty.

We tried getting help with another family therapist. This time I made various attempts at getting myself heard. When I interrupted, I was told "You are not polite, you're intrusive, you are not listening!" When I shouted that I had to speak, I was told, "You are angry."

It was fortunate for me these sessions were tape-recorded. I could document for myself that he used three quarters of each hour. Instead of feeling crazy, I felt validated.

My feelings of being trapped and cornered led me to rage and tears. While thus being gagged, I was simultaneously told I was beautiful, talented, sensual, and that he loved and wanted me. By putting me on such a pedestal, he was keeping me in my place (another familiar place for many women).

I finally realized what should have been apparent years before: my husband liked the marriage relationship when I was living my life through and for him. He couldn't hear what a real toll this situation had taken on me. I was told I was

selfish for wanting more for myself. How many women have heard they are selfish when they don't give of themselves 100% of the time? I was being driven crazy by a double message: his *words* were "develop your own interests, your own selfhood." Yet his *actions* and nonverbal communications were punishing me for being interested in my own life and effective at what I was doing.

Wanting more for myself was extremely threatening to my husband and our marriage system, which in turn made him more controlling and intimidating. The end of our marriage occurred when I found my anger at his trying to keep me in the one-down position. It was incredible to discover, within myself and within him, that what was once a deep and sensitive love and caring could turn to such distrust, contempt, and hate. I had never experienced rage before. I was shocked — since I am a mild-tempered, trusting person — to find I can be provoked to distrust and violent anger. A lot of my hostile feelings toward this particular man were provoked by the ways he dealt with me. Some of my angry feelings were aimed at society for creating such an unequal world.

My anger gave me the energy — a life-saving force, I'd say — to pull out of the relationship. Our divorce, in my opinion, was a product of our inability or unwillingness to work ourselves out of an unequal situation. The person who has a "good deal" in any system is going to be reluctant to change. I chose the only road to psychic survival.

Some marriages make it through the identity crises. Some do not. In my present counseling practice, I am keenly sensitive to women and men who are growing to new selfhood, and how this shakes up established patterns in a relationship.

Part Two

Sex Roles During
Separation and Divorce

The See-Saw:
Disorientation/Exhilaration

When I first separated, I moved out of the home I had helped to design—the home where I knew for sure that I was an important mother-person. I had asked my husband to vacate the house, but he refused. In the long run, he did me a favor. Since I was the one who had changed, become unhappy with the relationship, the necessary first step of separating was up to me. In anticipating the move, I had many nights of cold sweat and nightmares. It was like wrenching myself from my own womb.

I can't believe this is me . . .that I did it! I have actually pulled out of our house and away from my children. I'm in a state of shock, I think. This house is pleasant enough, but how strange to be living with someone else's furnishings, decor, smells, and sounds. The emptiness is overwhelming. Where are the children, hassling or needing to be listened to? Who do I kiss goodnight? Have I ever gone to bed in a strange house, alone, before? No.

I wander around aimlessly, studying the knickknacks of the family whose house this is. Oriental rug, Indian vase, saffron on the spice shelf—new items to live with, for me.

How can I make this space feel like me? How can I help the children feel this is their second home? Will they come and be with me? Will I ever have breakfast with them again? As I write this I sob. I feel totally cut off from who and what I am—the mother, wife, housekeeper, party-planner, birthday-party giver, counselor to children and husband, me. I have a desolate feeling of aloneness. I don't want to go to bed until I am so exhausted I'll have no trouble sleeping.

The strain of finding this place—the house or apartment hunt—shows on my face. I'm tense and tired. When I first started hunting, I felt so guilty I looked at very cheap, dumpy places, thinking that was all I deserved or all we could afford. Then I wondered what my husband would do if he was the one looking for a temporary dwelling. "Why, he would find himself a nice place that the kids could visit!" I say to myself. And I changed my tack.

I got tired of telling landlords, "I'm separating from my husband. My children will be visiting me." It was hard to say it without bursting into tears. Little do they know the agony behind that statement. They look critical, like, "Can you pay your bills?" or "Are you abandoning your children?" Ugh! Heavy feeling!

To live alone, even for five months, was an awakening experience. Although the pain of not being the major parent-caretaker never left me during those months, I was amazed to discover that I spent many hours of the evening just soaring with the emotional relief and a new sense of self.

So much of my existence had been focused on serving others, this aloneness was like plugging myself into an electric energy circuit. I had only myself to answer to. I loved having my own rooms. I played records and let my body move to the rhythm.

Last night I put on some records and danced. I felt the freedom of being here, of being *me*. To move my body to the rhythm of the blues, or jazz, or even some classical music, put me in touch with my vitality. I really need to touch my own body to know I am here.

At the same time I was disoriented: Who am I? Where am I? What day is it? I was lonely—particularly for my children—and had nightmares about their safety. I worried they would never forgive me or never be really connected to me again. To not be with them was torment.

> "God, this morning when I woke up, it took me ten minutes—yes, ten minutes—to figure out where I was. Weird. In my half-awake state (I think I didn't want to wake up), I tried to figure out where the windows would be in the room if I opened my eyes. Without my routine of seeing the girls through breakfast, and getting them off to school, I didn't care if this day began.
>
> Fortunately today is one of the days I have to go to my job. So I have to get up! I wander around the empty house looking at rooms filled with toys belonging to someone else's kids. A stuffed doll, Dr. Seuss books, a clown's face on the wall.
>
> I go into the kitchen where some other woman collects her favorite utensils. No egg poacher. Damn! The toaster doesn't work. Tears roll down my face as I eat untoasted bread with jelly. I'm resisting calling "home" to see if the kids packed their sandwiches for school, or if they missed me last night.
>
> It must be very strange for them to get up and realize I am not there. Does it hurt them as much as it hurts me? Good Lord—the one thing I do not want is to be separated from them. But for now it seems like the only solution.

After five months of legal battle, I regained my home territory and learned a lot about myself in the process.

After I had lived for months away from our family home, the lawyers persuaded my husband to move out and let me return. Did he agree to this because of his plans to remarry? Or his hopes that he and I might re-unite? Or legal reasons? Or because the girls wanted me back in the nest? Probably a combination of all of these reasons, but I'm not sure. It was painful for him to pack up and leave. We both loved the house and the warm memories it held.

Power and Control

The divorce procedures are not my focus since there are thousands of such painful stories. It is the sex roles in our marriage and divorce that I am reviewing.

During the process of divorce—a year and a half—the big issue was control. Who calls the shots? Who is in charge? Who has the power? Month after month I found that in each part of our settlement I had to prove I was correct in order to get what was due. It was similar to being perceived guilty until proved innocent. Since he had the income, the credit, the power, I had to argue and fight to get my fair share *from* him. He was fighting to protect what was "his." He was "giving." I was "taking." Why? We had both brought money and energy into the marriage. Each of us had worked very hard. The difference was that I had not received an income, or status, for my work.

The following is an episode where I played out my role.

Dressed to look "beautiful" in a soft blue wool suit, I sit with legs enticingly crossed as I keep my thoughts to myself amidst four men: three lawyers—his, mine, and an arbitrator—and my husband.

"There he is," I ponder, "the man with whom I used to make love, the man I confided in, listened to, played with, and with whom I had three children. Where did it all go?"

He is sitting in a straight-back chair holding pages of single-spaced, tightly handwritten notes. His legs crossed in a protective gesture, his arms folded to lessen his trembling, he reads page after page of *his* interpretation of our divorce.

"She wanted her independence, so I *gave* it to her, at great grief and pain to me."

I mumble to myself, "What I want is the right to be me, to my personhood!"

My lawyer leans over, touches my arm in a gesture which says, "Keep quiet, don't say a word."

On my husband drones, describing what a fine father he is and how I ruined the marriage.

Is this for my benefit or to gain some legal advantage. I'm not sure. I stay mute. Four men are giving the final verdic after all of this battle. Even though I have felt supported by my lawyer, the lack of another female in the room is overwhelming.

"Stay cool, be sweet and pretty, look pained, do it like they do in the movies," I keep telling myself. "It will all be over soon. Give them what they want." I feel raped. Silence is the only way I can be heard.

Divorce: A Stigma

I am sure there is much written about being newly single and all that it implies. I won't dwell on it except to say that I fel the shame that society places on a divorced woman (much more than a divorced man). Instead of the puritanical "A" for Adultery which was sewed on a woman's front, I felt there was a capital "D" on my back, for DIVORCED. In my supermarket one day, I overheard a man saying to another man "Come on over tonight, Joe. My wife and I are having a divorcée over for supper, and boy, she is really hot to trot Come join the fun!" I thought, "So that's how these upper class Yankee townsmen feel about the newly single woman." I wanted out.

I had very few close friends of my own, since most of our relationships had been through my husband. I was immediately cut off from couples' gatherings except for three favorite couples who told me that their friendship with us as a couple had basically been because of their linkage with me. Fortunately for me, they were not threatened by my singleness. An occasional threesome to the movies or dinner was fun for them, too. My husband, on the other hand, was taken in by couples and families. He was invited out to dinner; people brought in food for him and the kids; women came in to cook his meals. Society tends to heap pity and concern on a man and to ostracize the separated woman. I know—I've been on both sides: ignoring the separated woman while taking her spouse under my wing, and being ostracized myself.

One of my woman friends was kind enough to tell me that my separation was terribly threatening to her, since she had contemplated the same type of move. At least she let me know why I was not invited to dinner at her house (although she invited my husband).

But none of the shame or aloneness dampened the exhilaration of self-discovery and a sense of new strength. I feel sure that many people can make this rediscovery within a marriage. My situation prevented that.

Return to Square One

Learning the strange qualities of the social scene of the newly single woman was sometimes fun, sometimes ridiculous, and often painful. I felt shy, strange, uncomfortable, foolish, adolescent, in facing all the old issues of how to relate to men, how to handle the dating scene after nineteen years with one man. I learned to pick up the phone and take the initiative in asking a man to lunch or to come for a walk on a moonlit eve. It was strange to have my teenaged daughters watch and support me in my new ventures, as well as laugh at my timidity in sharing the details with them.

After nineteen years with one man, the task of knowing anyone else intimately seems impossible. I am starting back at square one. Strange how being "free" changes the whole picture. I've had men friends—"our" friends. Now when I go to a party unattached, I'm *looking* for someone and they are looking, too. The sexual lights are flashing, "Stop, Go, Caution!"

He suggests we meet at a small jazz place, downtown. Not wanting to appear old-fashioned, I agree. But as I am driving alone at night, I feel lonely. I'll have to drive myself home late at night, also. A new, uncomfortable feeling.

I can't see a single face. Panic sets in. "What if he isn't here? I won't sit in this place alone, that's for sure! Maybe I'll just turn around and go home before it's too late." Then his smooth

voice curls into my ear as an arm slips around my waist. "W
are over here," he says as he leads me to a corner, and w
crunch onto a leather sofa. I am introduced to more people
can't see. On the dance floor my knees shake, and swea
trickles down my arm. "Good God," I say to myself, "I'm no
fifteen! He knows I'm nervous, and I wish he didn't. It's no
the same as at the party. I don't feel safe, here. Safe? Fron
what? Him? But I like him. He seems like a thoughtful
competent, tender man. And angry? Is it because I'm sexuall
attracted to him? Of course, that's part of it. But so what? M
body is telling me I'm scared and insecure. Is it because he i
Black? It didn't matter at the party. Does it now? I don't thin
so. I'm confused. And he is telling me to relax, which, o
course, I wish I could.

Then later: "Do I ask him in? To my house with no one i
it? Do I kiss him goodnight? What would it be like to sleep wit
him? Is that his mood? Is that too easy?" Same old question
just twenty years later!

I am ashamed to admit to my daughters that I am in thi
position. But when I tell them a small portion of it, the
encourage me to tell more and to try again. What incredibl
kids! I would think they would laugh at me. Or feel I wa
betraying them by being with someone other than their father.

It was important to me that I be sure of my own worth
whether or not I had a man at my side. Culturally, I had
experienced the message that a woman without an escort wa
to be pitied. In high school and college the girl without a date
was pitied and typed "unpopular." There were (and are
places she could not go without an escort. Or if she did, sh
was considered either strange, asking for trouble, o
aggressive.

My own sexist attitudes became clear when I saw a lovely
woman sitting in a fine dining room eating alone. I felt sorry
for her. Obviously, then, if *I* am eating alone (which is torture
for me), I am imagining others are pitying me. To overcome
this ingrained response—to feel worthy as a person without a
male partner—is not only an internal struggle, it is a battle
against the mores of our culture. As soon as I am able to

change my attitude about that solitary woman eating her meal, I will feel greater self-respect when I am alone. And if headwaiters would dignify us and men would stop harassing us when we are alone, the task would become much easier!

My most excruciating experiences were going to PTA or school functions where we had been known as "parents." Sitting alone in the auditorium as I listened to the Christmas choir or wandering through the halls on "back to school" night, I felt ostracism in the air. (Or was I imagining it?) Most couples seemed either overly polite or cool.

To fill my needs for friendship and intimacy, I had to reach out. I realized that I could not sit home alone and expect friendships to develop. It was in the process of extending myself to people, making a wide range of friends, that I slowly wiped away the concept that a woman is not complete without a partner. My life was full. Probably a group of friends will never completely fill my needs for intimacy and love, but my life can be joyful without "The Man."

I wanted new acquaintances and gaiety. I wanted music and dancing—a party where people would move and touch and laugh. I was used to gatherings where the whole evening was devoted to political talk. So I tried it! I wondered at first if I could manage a party like that on my own. I designed an invitation that let people know there would be a light mood. It said, "Bring your friends." They did. As the sun was coming up and the last people were leaving, I recalled how anxious and fearful I had felt just a few hours before, wondering if anyone would come—would it be fun? I had tried something new, and found again, "I can do it if I try!" Halloween costume parties, staff gatherings, potluck suppers, a yoga class— I opened my home to many people. I changed my style of entertaining completely. No more formal dinners, where I waited on people. It was "Come and bring somebody and something, and we will share it." It was fun for all of us, including the times when my daughters joined in.

It was incredible to me how my life changed in such beautiful ways in two years. In the same house, and the same town, and I had a new life!

Earning Power

Then the power of money came crashing in on me. All I had ever earned was $4,000, and we had been living at ten times that rate. I was terrified I would not be able to meet expenses. I had carefully budgeted our money when we were poor and happily spent most of what my husband earned when we were well off. For a few months, I toyed with the idea of walking away from the marriage without a fight for support. One of the ways my husband tried to intimidate me during our separation was to tell me I would not get any financial support, or custody of the children. I had to face whether I was willing to take that risk. In facing that fear, I gained strength. Again, it was my anger that gave me energy to fight for the chance to be supported temporarily while I upgraded my skills and earning power. In one sense, it was degrading to plead, beg, and fight (through my lawyer) for funds. On the other hand, I came to realize that I had worked for nineteen years for the benefit of a husband and children without any salary, and I deserved time and pay to establish myself professionally. At times, I would pace the floor and rage to myself, "Just once, just once, let him want something that *I have* that he wants. I will enjoy the revenge when he feels the demeaning process of asking for it." The only things I ever managed to *have* that he deeply wanted were my love letters to him. I cried and laughed as I sent them up in smoke.

So I learned the meaning of the power of those who have versus those who have not: money power. What had graciously been a "what is mine is yours" marriage became "what is ours is his" unless I fought.

My professional life and my relationships with my colleagues became increasingly important to me. During the year of my personal trauma, I invested new energy in my job as a psychotherapist for disturbed children, initiating parent groups and consultation to the teachers in addition to my individual and group therapy work with the children.

Ironically, the same month I got divorced, I was also fired from my job. My more assertive abilities were evident in my responses. A new director of the school found my competence and closeness to students, teachers, and parents too threatening to tolerate. He had chosen to cut back the scope of my professional functioning in a way that was humiliating and demeaning to me. I told him I would not do an inadequate job to please him. He told me to resign. I refused. He fired me. It was my first lesson as a newly emerging professional that some people are incapable of tolerating a competent woman. In years past, I would have acquiesced to his demands. No more!

I was without a partner, without a job, without much self-confidence, and with only a few close friends. I would stare at the phone for ten minutes before taking the risk of calling someone for a job lead, for friendship, for courage. Although there were a lot of "no jobs today" replies, I began to enjoy the interviews. I asked to be interviewed even if there was no possibility of a job. I learned about the various agencies and institutions—which later became good referral and resource information. I learned not to put myself down, to talk about my good points, my areas of competency. Essentially, I was learning: keep taking risks; take initiative; be honest, open; people do respond. After three months, I found a job.

During this time, I also signed up for workshops where I could learn new skills and make new friends. My ability to think and create, my competencies in the work I wanted to do—these became paramount to me. Before, working had always been an avocation. Devoting a good portion of my psychic energy to my job was a new and exciting experience.

Emerging: A Process of Change

How did I change both my circumstances and self-concept? Women ask me this. Suddenly I am no longer the woman looking for the way out of the maze, but the one who is looked to as a role model. This sudden shift floors me. Knowing that other women are desperately looking for ways out of their dilemmas inspires me to talk about what I have learned so far.

My husband and I were a man and a woman coming together with values favoring harmony, openness, togetherness, and joy in parenting. This context accentuates, I believe, the pathos of the episodes I have described.

Looking back on my nineteen years of marriage, I can now see I had been expected to play these roles:

A wife gets gratification through the life of her husband.

A wife protects and enhances the man's time to think, write, and solve the problems of the world.

A wife takes full charge of the young children's emotional and social development. Husbands get to play with the kids.

If a wife gets further education, this is a "gift" to keep her from discontent—she is not expected to be an equal force in the world.

If the marriage isn't working, it is the wife's fault. She should make things smooth and pleasant.

Avoid conflict! If there is a disagreement, particularly in ideology or in the intellectual sphere, flatter the male by conceding. "It isn't worth fighting about."

A wife gets "cared for" by allowing the husband to deal with the outside world, thus atrophying her assertive qualities in that world.

Getting out from under the sex role expectations helped release much of my creative energy. I do not need to accept for myself the notions that a woman should: accommodate, serve, live her life through a man, relinquish power to direct (in a leadership sense), look for male approval, soft-pedal intelligence, withdraw instead of confront people with anger, or find indirect ways of getting needs met.

The experiences I have been relating—the role expectations of childhood, marriage, divorce, and separation—must be viewed in the context of our times.

The women's movement was the backdrop for my scene. However, I had never read any books on women. *The Feminine Mystique* looked like a criticism of everything I believed in, so I never opened it. I was too frightened to join any consciousness-raising group, fearing I would become "unfeminine." Even the League of Women Voters seemed shallow because it was all female. My opinion of women was low, and I did not connect this with my own low self-esteem. It wasn't until I was separated that I really listened to experiences of other women. Listening always changes me.

The era of our marriage—1950–1970—is also a context for our difficulties. Men were MEN and women were "girls." Sex role expectations were at their height, and the women's movement was just beginning to educate us to our oppression.

Knowing *how* to change to enable women to have a place in the sun is not easy. I am reminded of Holly Near's song, "Free to Grow." "There must be something in your manly way that keeps her down. . . . I've never found a man who would do it for me! I've never found a man who could wait while I was free to grow." (And I still choke up each time I hear it.) She introduces the song this way: "It must be a hard time to be a white male. I think it's going to get better . . . . You see, women and racial minorities and children have been havin' such a hard time for soooo long, it's gotta get changed! In the meanwhile, change doesn't feel so good. But when we come through it on the other side, everybody is going to have more room where they are Free to Grow."

Over the years of writing this chapter—and the writing process itself has been part of my change process—I have evolved from blaming him for almost everything to understanding the impact society had on each of us as we were expected to act out the alienating male/female roles. And now I take responsibility for what I allowed to happen to me.

I know that his attitudes and actions had a great impact on me. I now also know, however, that our difficulties were caused in part by the social system or context—the lack of equality for women. And out of my own lack of awareness, I allowed myself to be put in the one-down position. I hid behind his image while he thrived on my support.

The process of my own change—from accusation to acceptance of what I allowed to happen to me, and anger at the system we have created—has been gradual. Listening to women, reading, writing my own journal, writing this book, and sharing my experiences have been important parts of the metamorphosis. And I am not through yet!

There are also some guidelines I have developed for myself:

I have to take responsibility for my own life.

I need to take risks.

I need to be aware of myself: my body and my feelings.

I need to be open to my intuition.

I need to know how and when to reveal myself.

I need to find or create a support group.

I can design my own personal change and transitions.

I will expand on each of these points.

I have learned over and over again that I have to take responsibility for my own life. There have been many times, and I am sure there will be many more, when I have felt truly frightened and alone. I've looked at myself in the mirror and said, "Natalie, if you don't take care of yourself, no one will. If you don't like yourself, no one will." I have the ability to create and design my own life. Though that creation must take into account the effect on many other lives, what I am and what I do is up to me. I understand now that, despite an unequal partnership and an oppressive society of which I was a part, there is much of my life I can alter by changing *myself.*

Although there are specific second-class roles for women and although there are individuals who will try to intimidate me or put me down, it is *me* that allows myself to feel demeaned. When I am aware of my own reactions and feelings, I am much more able to take charge of myself and fight in constructive ways.

I have learned the meaning of taking risks. There have been a lot of "firsts" in the past few years, each one accompanied by fear, self-doubt, and loneliness. There was the first time I planned a vacation by myself with and without my daughters, the first dates, the first lover, the first long-term relationship with another man, the first rejection, the first time I ran a therapy group on my own, the first time I was a solo paid consultant, the first time I chose to join a politically oriented training group for group leaders. There has been pain as well as exhilaration in each of those risks. As long as I live and learn deeply in each experience, I am satisfied.

It is also important to me to take time to be aware of myself, including the messages my body is sending me. Self-awareness is the road to conscious choice in our behavior. If I am aware I am angry, I can choose to shout or write or take political action. If I am aware I am sad, I can find someone to talk to who will let me cry, or go jogging as a release. But if these feelings are not in my awareness, they take control of me, and I am in a state of confusion or anxiety.

To be open to my intuitive feelings, to dream, to fantasize, to play with ideas of what I would most want in my life if I waved a magic wand—this opening of the mind to options is helpful to me. When I counsel people, I also try to help them play this game. Women, particularly, have limited their vision in this culture and thus have limited their choices.

Knowing how and when to reveal myself is always a struggle. It seems significant to me that ten years ago, en route to my first five-day encounter group, I was reading Sidney Jourard's *The Transparent Self.* In the margin I wrote notes to myself, saying, "Self-disclosure is okay for *other* people, but not for me!" I have learned much since then about how, when, and to whom I can be open.

I need to find or create a support group. Having been an extremely private person, it was a new and painfully slow lesson that letting myself be known was the road to emotional closeness. To know that I can count on some people to be with me through tears, angers, frustrations, and confusion, as well as to share in my joys, is truly important.

Designing personal transitions in life has a special meaning to me, since I have made several major changes in my life. I have learned that I can create for myself and others a place where ideas and warmth can flourish. I have a sense of my own power to create, influence, and make happen. I am the captain of my own ship, me!

...ys build planes and become pilots. Girls learn to be charming, sweet, and ...vely. Boys stretch their muscles, increase their skills, and aim. Girls wear ...othes which restrict their bodies and activities.

*Looking the world in the eye.
At a woman's college the
frustration of holding myself in
check intellectually was gone.*

*Entering matrimony, eyes cast
down, legs crossed, demure and
subservient. The role is cast.*

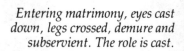

2
Uprooting and Rerooting
A Transition

I am about to make another major shift in my life. I have chosen to pull up my taproot, to leave my East Coast home of twenty years, knowing that my children have left the nest, and that I will create a place for them wherever I am. I am about to leave my support group: people who have nourished me and to whom I have given much. I will move 3,000 miles and start a new life—design my own work, make new friends, and shed some of the material possessions I have acquired over the years. It feels like a tremendous leap into the unknown.

In this chapter there is one theme which is sometimes stated forcibly, and at other times heard only in muted form. It is the constant inner struggle to allow the masculine and feminine parts of myself to emerge in ways that integrate my life. I hope you understand that I am not referring to the stereotyped "male" or "female" in our society, but to the essential dichotomy within each of us.

My masculine side is evident as the adventurous, risk-taking, assertive part of myself: the me that puts carbon paper under my personal letters so that I will have a sense of my own history; the me that tries to draw personal, cognitive conclusions from that history. It is the social activist and doer.

My feminine side is my creative energy, my openness and receptivity, my feelings—whether warm, hot, or cold— my intuitive awareness, my sensitivity. It is the me that wants to do nothing more than *be* in nature, taking in the smells, sights, sounds, and movement of the universe. It is the me that would prefer not to speak, but to relate to people in a sensual, non-verbal way.

This theme of opposition and fusion is evident throughout my process of making a decision to move: in building a

47

bridge to the West Coast, in learning how to say farewell, and in my rerooting in California.

The Decision

Although I am planful, there are no plans; decisions seem to happen before I have fully committed myself to them. How can a decision be made without my consciously making it? When I review what led up to my move from East to West Coast I see that I was combining both the logical, linear, masculine side of me and the intuitive, receptive, female side.

I had spent the summer in California working and playing, taking in the smells, sights, sounds as well as the informality and openness of the people. These impressions struck a chord deep inside me. I was using both my conscious and unconscious to gather information.

When I returned to my home near Boston I realized the decision had been made. A maple tree growing beside our house helped me see the course my life had taken. I had planted it years earlier. Its roots had gone deep. I had watched it grow from sapling to a mature tree, and the broad leaves were now giving much shade to the roof. There were many roots and rich memories in this place for me; yet I needed to get out from under that cool shade of my previous life into the light of a new one.

Following my divorce I had seriously considered leaving my home of twenty years several times. In fact, I had come close to leaving the previous year. At that time, many things happened that told me the time was not right. I had tried to find a job in California by mail. No luck. I had written a letter to my ex-husband that I was going to leave with our youngest daughter, Naomi. He threatened to take me to court to fight for her. I had checked it out with Naomi by saying, "How you feel about moving will influence me, but will not be the controlling factor. I want to do what is right for me, but having you happy is also very important to me." As I struggled with the decision, I also realized how much I would miss my other two daughters. I tried to be receptive to my feelings, the facts, the over-all vibes. The pieces of the puzzle were not fitting together. Something about the situation didn't feel good. The time was not right.

How, a year and a half later, did the time become right? There were several factors: I was becoming painfully aware of the "empty nest" syndrome—a response which occurs in women who have invested a major part of their emotional energy in the rearing of children when the children leave home. Women who have done little else outside the home seem more seriously affected, even when they have had avocations or part-time jobs. However, even women who are very excited about their careers seem deeply affected when their children leave home. It occurred to me that I could leave our nest at the same time my youngest daughter graduated from high school. I could actively help myself avoid my sense of loss.

I wrote this in June, and my women friends who have their last child graduating from high school were suffering. These are women who have had careers, so they have not been living a life through or for their children. Yet the pain of separation is real, and it is great. It is not, "What will I do with my life without them?" The feeling seems to be, "An important part of me, of my identity, is no longer needed." And the need to be needed is a large part of most mothers' identity. Symbolically, that need is surgically removed when the last child graduates. I say surgically because we as mothers have not said, "This is a part of me I now want to cast aside." It happens *to* us. The separation is inflicted upon us, whether we are ready for it or not. It is also true that as June and graduation of the youngest child occurs, mothers feel a tremendous sense of release and freedom.

The lack of education and preparation for women on this issue enrages me. We have no ritual in this society to integrate the necessary grief and joy a mother feels at this time. We as mothers are supposed to pretend that nothing much has happened. If we admit that the passage of children into adult life is a joyous occasion for parents and that we are glad to have them leave, we are looked upon as lacking in some basic mothering quality. For the children, this may be a time when they feel elated over a new sense of independence, or rejected and cut off from their lifeline, or a combination of both. It seems to me it is a time to re-assess the relationship and look at who needs whom, how much, and why. It can be a time to be honest about giving and taking, about needs for privacy and shared intimacy. It is a time when children and parents can, if they wish, become more like friends. How nice it would be to have mothers (and fathers, if they wish to join in) celebrate the beginning of a new period in their lives, and put in perspective their feelings of separation from children and rebirth of self!

In my own way, I had been actively preparing for the sense of loss when my girls were on their own. I was still aware that I could avoid developing my own potential by constantly waiting for their return, even if it was just for the day, or a week, or a summer. I see it happen: women spend a lot of time preparing for daily events and waiting for them to happen. We prepare the house and the evening meal and wait for husband and children to come home. Even though we may be busy cooking or cleaning or reading, there is a feeling of waiting for someone. When those persons are gone through graduation, trips away, divorce, death, or any other reason, we are with the waiting feeling, since our lives have been centered on doing for those others.

So, instead of waiting, I wanted to position myself for developing my own life. That seemed to be, by all cultural standards, "selfish." I was afraid I would hear people charge or insinuate "How *could* you dismantle the home that had been full of love and closeness for many years and was security midst turmoil for your children during the last few rough years? How could you *not* put their needs first?" I know that had internalized many of those values and had to talk myself out of them, with the help of my children and friends. My greatest problem, initially, was approaching my daughters with the possibility of my move. I was carrying the guilt of feeling "selfish" (to say nothing of facing my own feelings of loss, knowing that they would be on the East Coast as I moved

West). But as usual, they were the best ones to consult. I received clear statements from them that I needed to do what felt right for me: "Yes, we will miss you . . . .no, we don't *want* you to go . . . .yes, we think you should go if you want . . . .-no, I won't go with you, but I will love you and visit you . . . .maybe I'll go to school out there, maybe I won't . . ." All of these words came tumbling out and we hashed and rehashed them until I became more comfortable (and they became tired of my needing to ask).

I looked forward to living in a place where my history as a "wife" was not known. Having lived a lot of my nineteen years of marriage with my identity as Mrs. _____, the wife of _____, I was tired of fighting for my new identity. In a new locale, I could just *form* it. Also, I was aware of the constant competition my ex-husband and I had over our children. Our family therapist had commented once that some marriages get in trouble over who is the best parent. I also felt competitive over our life styles and our values. With children shifting through two households, the news of who was doing what and why (although kept to a minimum), was a constant irritant to my competitive self. I was curious about his new life, yet I did not want to know. I wanted him to know how well I was doing on my own, yet I wanted it kept secret. I wanted the girls to feel free to say anything about either of us, yet I frequently felt like shouting "I *don't* want to hear about . . ." or "Don't say anything about . . . ."

My need to *prove* myself, to be better, to show him—all seem like an admission of great pettiness—yet, damn it, those feelings were very real! I flash on the song: "I can do anything better than you can. I can do ANYTHING better than YOU! (NO, YOU CAN'T!) Yes, I CAN!"

I'm sure this feeling dates back to *all* of what I felt as a female growing up in this society as I deferred to men and let them take credit for all important accomplishments. I was reacting to father, brother, and the men who are in charge of the world, as well as my husband.

So, in leaving the territory my husband and I both shared for many years, I was hoping to leave a lot of the constant competition over children, lifestyles, personal achievement and worth. I was also acknowledging that my parenta role would soon have different dimensions. My dream involved starting afresh, allowing new aspects of mysel to emerge, wondering what I could become—personally an professionally.

One of the most helpful things to me in making th decision to leave was the way in which my Greenhous friends helped me look at my leaving. This was a group o fifteen people with whom I had received professional training We worked as a counseling collective. As I gingerly broache the subject to them, fearful that they would be angry at m possible departure, they let me know I would be sorel missed, but they would help me do, in a positive way, wha was right for me. I had toyed with the idea of not telling then until a few weeks before leaving, as a way of being "kind" (o as a way of not dealing with how they would feel). I would jus sort of say, "Oh, by the way, I'm leaving for good next week, give everyone a hug and walk out. My twisted notion at tha moment was that it would be easier for all of us that way However, my inner turmoil over the process of uprooting wa so great, I *needed* their suggestions and support and I couldn' keep my tears, dreams, and plans to myself. Their reactio was: "We need the six months' time to prepare ourselve emotionally for your leaving. We want to help you think abou the new organization that you are building on the West Coast and hope that a bridge will be made between us, eventually. Their support allowed me to be excited about my possibl future. They let me dream out loud and joined in my excite ment while saying they were envious about my venture, sa (not angry) about my leaving, and excited by my enthusiasm The realness of their emotions felt very supportive. It helpe me feel both my excitement and my sadness.

Someplace in my unconscious lurked the question, "Wi you—any or all of you—reject me or get rid of me before leave you?" In retrospect, I can see the reason I asked, "Wi you be angry at me for leaving?" My fear of being closed out c turned off during my last six months was great. I found it di

ot happen. By being *aware* of this fear of rejection, I think I did
hings to make sure it would *not* happen. Instead of gradually
ading from the Boston scene, I involved myself intensely with
eople and projects. My energy and emotions were high.

I don't often write down dreams, but one I had was so
uzzling and disturbing that it is in my journal. At the time of
he dream I was considering leaving a job I liked because the
ersonality and incompetence of the top man was such that I
oresaw the possibility of the institution sinking. (It did.) This
ream seems relevant to my various processes of leaving:
eaving a marriage, leaving a job, and leaving my home.

Part One: I am standing in my back yard; there are young,
attractive, "hip" friends around me. We are trying to trans-
plant a big white-barked tree. "It is a boxwood tree," I say.
(Why is that? I'm not sure there is such a tree, and I've never
seen one.) We gather around. The tree is slanting off to the left
at an angle. There are also graceful branches leaning to the left.
There are catkins—soft, pussy-willow catkins in bouquet-like
bunches dangling from the tree. We are urgently trying to
move the tree, trying to get up all the roots to go with it. There
is some danger we will be disrupted or found out. Someone
does not want it moved!

Part Two: There is a very angry man present. He has his
arm stretched out, with a fist at my face. It is a long arm, and it
comes close to my face, threatening me. My arm is also
stretched long with a fist at his face. But my arm is shorter, so
his fist is *much* closer to my face than mine is to his.

Part Three: There is a big piece of furniture (I'm not sure
what) in my house that has to be moved out—very urgently.
My young friends are trying to help me. They have to open the
wall in my bedroom to move out this heavy furniture. The
window wall is partly removed and the heavy object goes onto
the big van in the front yard. It rushes away. Then my friends
go to the back yard, get into their various old beat-up sports
cars and try to escape via a muddy road down by the creek.
They step on the gas, wheels spin and they get stuck and slide
around and eventually zoom off with a loud noise.

At the time of this dream, I was in the process of "leaving the system," and the dream made enough impact to help me get out. That system was one in which the boss was devious, manipulative, an empire builder, and a liar (the angry man). The staff within the institution were effective, warm, creative young women and men. So I have a lot of associations from this dream with that job. As I read the dream now, however, it resonates for me on many levels echoing my *leaving:* separation from my marriage (the man with repressed rage and threatening fist) and leaving my home.

I associate the left angle of the boxwood tree with my spiritual, intuitive, left side, which is graceful. This is my feminine self. I also associate it with my "left" leaning politically and my association with the Greenhouse collective.

Trying to get up all the roots of the tree feels like me trying to take my daughters with me wherever I go. The angry man with whom I am angry, is both my ex-husband and the boss. am aware of feeling powerless, yet struggling to feel my own power by putting my fist out. By being assertive and confronting (which I had been in both cases), I may possibly get clobbered (I did in one instance).

Having the piece of furniture moved out via the bedroom seems symbolic. My first move toward separation from my husband was to leave the marriage bed. Moving him out through the bedroom wall is an appropriate image.

So the dream is fused with many parting symbols, much of which I may not see, even now. It is a dream of uprooting and rerooting. During the dream I was intensely anxious and fearful.

In making my decision I tried to be open to different forms of information: to my feelings, to the feelings of my children and friends, to my intuitive sense and my dreams as well as my logical mind. When logic and intuition did not mesh, I stayed. When all the energy coming in seemed to say "go," I was able to leave.

Leaving the security of the known to leap into the unknown is always frightening. These major transitions in my life—my divorce, job change, and my move—were anxious times. A sense of impending danger, of bewilderment and disorientation are part of all my leavings.

On the other hand, I was excited by my fantasies of starting life in a new place. My anticipation was high. Spontaneity, freedom, creating a new life with my new identity, living closer to nature in a warmer climate, a sense of personal pioneering and self-confidence, a wish to build the kind of work situation in a geographic area that might accept my new notions with more alacrity—these were the bright feelings I experienced.

Yet, I was frequently wrought-up with unexplained anxiety and terror, totally out of proportion to the situation. Fears of super-calamity and catastrophe plagued me. I was hesitant to share the daytime "nightmares" that churned inside me. They seemed so stupid and unnecessary. Yet, there they were: "I'll never see my children again!" (The worst possible calamity.) "I'll die in a plane crash!" "I'll get murdered in the street!" "I'll be a total failure and be hungry and alone!"

When I looked more intently at the worst fear—that I would never see my children again—it was obvious that the literal translation of that fear was nonsense. But the underlying terror was that physical distance would sever the meaningfulness of our relationships. My friend, Dee, listened to the depths of that pain, reassuring me that if I worked at it, the relationships with adult children would be good in quality, even though the quantity would be less.

Sometimes I was my own worst enemy as I got angry at myself for *having* such exaggerated and ridiculous emotions. Gradually, as I let a few close friends know what I was living through, I found these anxieties were a normal part of most persons' kaleidoscopic repertoire during the process of making a decision. I tried to accept and forgive myself for being thunder, storm, and lightning as well as rainbow.

In the process, I learned to trust my inner sense about the right time to make a change. I learned that I need to reveal my dreams of the future and my mournfulness about parting. The words "support group" seem too cold and impersonal to describe my friends and children as they helped my decision emerge.

Building a Bridge

The process of building a personal bridge to the West Coast evolved over two or three years. My parents had lived in California for many years, and my trips to visit them had given me the sense that I would feel at home in the West (although I chose northern California rather than their southern area). I spent two summers and one Christmas vacation in California testing whether it would be a good place for me. I went to an art therapy workshop and met people of interest, spent time driving up the coast, and explored the Bay Area. I felt the warmth of the climate, the drama of the coastline, and the informality and accepting attitude of many of the people. I felt I could happily fit in.

Having three close friends move into the Bay Area during those three years was also influential. Dee had courageously packed up her children and moved without a job in hand, which showed me that it could be done. Dick and Marion and I had dreamed of working together establishing a Center to help individuals and agencies plan their transitions. We had begun by becoming a non-profit organization on paper. Although this was not a security in terms of income, since we would have to create our own, it was an identity and direction for me.

I spent a couple of months living in a commune to see how I would like cooperative living. Would I ever be able to give up most of my possessions and live in one room with the rest of the space jointly owned and occupied by many others? Did I want to change my life that way? The time was well spent. I became aware of what personal needs I had and the kind of people I would want to live with. I was amazed to find that I was more flexible in my lifestyle than I had thought. It opened up options of how I could live—if I chose to do so.

There were some things I was willing to give up for a

more cooperative life, such as being the major domo in the kitchen, or having a living room that was "mine." But there were some things I needed for my psychic survival: a bedroom for myself large enough to sleep, write, and do yoga in. And I needed mature housemates of any age who were cooperative and communicative.

I called acquaintances and friends of friends and took the initiative to say hello, during my brief visits. I was putting out my antennae to see what the response would be. The reception felt warm. The message I picked up everywhere was, "Join us."

Learning How to Say Farewell

In looking back, I see that many activities during my last year or six months at home were unconsciously preparing me for departure. I was cherishing all that I had before leaving it. It felt like preparing for a kind of death; it was "you have six months to live *here*," rather than "you have six months to live." Some of the effect was the same:

I spent *more* time with the people I loved most.

I took time to do those things I had always said I'd do but never got around to.

I gave away meaningful objects—plants, clothes, pictures, a favorite table.

I took pictures of the places and people I was going to leave.

I organized some of my own farewell celebrations.

I took special note of my surroundings, knowing that I would be leaving the seasons with their dramatic changes. My camera was my recorder of what I loved in New England. A dramatic picture of the Concord River at sunset, a lighthouse at the Cape, apple blossoms in Weston, the bare winter branches of an oak tree, pine needles in the golden sunlight, milkweed pods unfolding—all came out of my sense of appreciation for what I was about to leave. Some of my best photographs happened during a walk around my own neighborhood, as I really took in what was there. In the process of saying goodbye, I was appreciating what was around me. It made day-to-day living bittersweet.

As for the people around me, I involved myself more, not less. I worked hard at being effective with my colleagues at Greenhouse. I had an intense physical-emotional relationship with a man, knowing and insisting it would end. I was aware of spending special time with my daughters—having their friends over, going to their performances in music and drama and having special birthday celebrations. Every time they would walk in the door, I'd say to myself, "Next month they won't be walking in the door, so take time and *be* with them."

The last month at home was incredible. Something was planned for every night of the month. I had never realized I had so many friends. It was a moving experience to find out how I had touched people's lives. My initial temptation was to pooh-pooh it—to say they don't really care about me that much. Then I really tried to accept what I was hearing.

A free-floating piece of writing that I did in my journal gives more of the flavor of the last two weeks at home:

> a crazy week...two weeks...how many days/nights, i dunno. i feel flooded with warmth and love from people: pat and jim and ruth and mike tonight. people who want me around and care. bright interesting, radical/liberal, traveling people who like me around for my energy. am i nuts to leave? will they come to me? i inspire them to new interests. they support me to go on!
>
> what a week! a loneliness talk with patsy reading her poetry. an m.i.t. group with patsy and me as the only women and the other bright writer/politico humans.
>
> what a week! clem and oriental june and henry the love with his julie all at a party for me? i dunno...but the last

soliloquy was about me and how i had introduced myself so personally at their forum that it set their whole meeting in tune with their personal goals . . .

what a week! then today, a picture of me came in the mail from r . . .a warm, black and white real wrinkles and smiles earthy picture. i dig it.

what a week! tomorrow s. comes and we'll say goodbye. it is so loaded for me i don't know where to begin. like, do i tell him that i have thought about him many, many hours and the pain i feel *for* him as well as the pain i have in leaving him? i'd like to tell him how many aches i have and the love i have for him.

. . .as my naomi said, "there will be many people who will miss you because you mean a lot to them, but you won't leave a hole in anyone's life." i find it hard to accept both of those things. i find it hard to say no one will miss me desperately, and no one will i miss desperately. it's that way, now. unless t. will miss me that much. he may. i'm sorry if that is true.

what a week! he left me daisies and a poem while i was out tonite. that was sweet. he has helped me in ways he won't ever know, in keeping me warm and real and responsive during this very hard time for me while i try to pick up and go.

and i am excited about going! really turned on to having my own space in s.f. and living alone for awhile to see what i'll create for myself! and worried about being lonely. but excited about filling my own space and time with dance and paint and finding out about a city and finding new people. i guess i know that there are good and warm people everywhere . . . .will i find them and they me? yes. they, i, will . . .i'll do it.

and will my girls come and be with me? yes, somehow they will . . .or i'll find my way back here.

will i come back here? will i?

On the last day of April I went to the lawyer's office and officially sold the house, went to the bank and invested the money, went home and hurriedly finished packing the boxes. I needed time, at that moment, to nurture my soul. I climbed into the bathtub to soak out the physical aches and soothe the emotional pains, before getting dressed to go to the plane. As I slid into the water, the movers arrived. Although I shouted at them to wait outside for ten minutes while I finished my bath, they walked right in. They swept the insides of my house right into the mouth of their mammoth truck in about an hour. All that was left when the truck pulled away was the shell. I tried not to look at the emptiness.

As I sat down to write this, I found I was still affected by the violation inherent in that scene, and the conflicts it embodied. There is the ever-present problem of taking care of my spirit and soul (taking a few luxurious moments to relax) when there is always so much I want to *do*. My need to be introspective, inward, meditative, and spiritual seems in constant conflict with my drive and ability to get things accomplished, be organized, efficient, and active. The assertive, masculine side of me is activist and raring to go. The feminine, receptive part of me wants to nurture myself and others and be alone in nature, creating beauty.

The movers walked in even when I had asked for my time alone (it was a new and courageous step for me to *ask*), just as the world we live in won't allow for the time we need to mourn, grieve, celebrate, or integrate and center ourselves. The movers move on!

Letting Go

I felt the pain of closing the door on the now vacant, barren house only fleetingly because my exhaustion and attention to other details prevailed. Fortunately, friends and my youngest daughter came to take me to dinner and put me on the plane. We were giddy and chattering, avoiding the ache and wrench of the parting. I got on the super-bird to fly west and plopped myself across four empty seats in the back with pillows and blankets, intending to take just a nap. Six hours later I awoke to the sound: "Fasten your seat belts. We are landing in San Francisco!" I couldn't believe I had slept the *whole* way. The strain of the last month was just beginning to tell on me. Sleeping was also a way of numbing myself after the final tug of pulling up the taproot. It was easier, perhaps, to move through this tunnel, this passageway or birth canal, if I kept my eyes closed and my senses turned off.

I looked out the window and said to myself, "This will be my new home! I wonder, wonder, how it will be?" It was three o'clock in the morning. My niece, Anne, roused herself from her medical school bed to come greet me. It was important to have someone I really loved there to welcome me. She deposited me at Dick and Marion's, where I tiptoed in and slept until dawn.

Typical of my high expectations of myself, I had thought I'd be settled and raring to go within twenty-four hours. Five days later I was still staggering around, catching up on sleep, feeling tremendous culture shock (which I knew a lot about from our Peace Corps days), and needing time alone without excessive demands. A community letter to friends and daughters back East shows how I felt:

Last night I wept and wept. From the depths of my tight-sore tummy (from holding it all in), I wept the tears of goodbye and farewell that I had not shed. It was all right. It was good. I was in the warmth of my three best friends, here, by the fireside, being held and massaged as the tears kept flowing. I talked, once in a while, between sobs. I spoke of you, and you and you, and of the goodbyes and things said and things left unsaid. I spoke of the last two and three months—of how many people had told me words of appreciation that I tried very hard to let in, because I know that I usually hold off such words—and how I wondered if I had ever really said back to you what I felt. Please know that you are important to me and that I have love to give you. Yes, this is a letter to many of you; and I love you in different ways, you know.

Last night I had visions of my empty house looking out at the hopa apple tree in pink full bloom without me there to admire it. Last night I felt the pain of giving up the home ground for three beautiful daughters who would come in to do laundry, to teach music, to sew and gab and laugh and get stoned, and to fight and bitch, share troubles and highlights. That still makes me cry. And I know the four of us will share

time and space together in new ways. And I know the time is right.

Today I am beginning to feel settled. My life seems like the scene out my window: there is mist and fog with a bright spot of sunshine on the distant hills. I am beginning to unwind and feel centered. I want to explore the city and reach out to new acquaintances. I have a fire in my fireplace, the warmth of your friendship, and the courage to be.

This letter describes the excruciating pain of letting go. To accept that what *was* will no longer *be* is extremely difficult. Although the time may be right to leave, that does not eliminate the agony of giving up a particular way of life. I was no longer a married woman nor the hub of the lives of three daughters. Letting go of the house, the symbol of "home"—as I let go of the need to be needed as a nested parent—was anguish. To surrender to that feeling through tears, outcries, sleep, and sleeplessness, was apparently a necessary step to letting go.

Limbo

In reading about transitions, and discussing with others their own changes, I have learned that being in the "no-where" for awhile is an important phase. Instinctively, I must have known this as I planned to have six weeks to myself to explore and discover and settle in. That "no-where," however, can be a very puzzling, chaotic, turbulent place of high peaks and deep valleys. A poem gives the gist of it:

California, CALIFORNIA!
I am warmly greeted.
(I am alone.)
I march out to meet each new situation.
(I am fearful and shy.)
I make my own world.
(A tough world exists.)
I feel new energy; a challenge.
(I long to hide.)
People feel my spirit—put out a hand.
(I reach; it disappears.)
Who am I?
NOW.

My fears were outrageous. I was often disoriented. Every morning, as my eyes would open, I'd lie in bed for awhile figuring out: Where am I? Who am I? What day is it? What month is it? What do I do first today? What do I need to do? What do I want to do? Does it matter? Who needs me?

When I look back on it, I can laugh at some of my ways of helping myself get oriented. I had maps of San Francisco over my sink *and* next to my desk *and* pasted on the inside of my front door so that I could look at them every time I left the apartment. *And* maps in my pocketbook; and, when I bought a car, I hung one from the dashboard! And yet, I am not an inexperienced traveler. I have been around the world, lived in Hawaii two separate years, lived in the Philippines in the city and in the barrio. Newness and change are things I crave, look forward to. They excite me. So what was so different about this move? Why was I feeling so lost, so scared? When I wanted to go to some part of the city by bus, I'd spend half an hour trying to figure out the bus route on the maps. When I was unloading groceries from my car and had to make two trips up the three flights to my apartment, I'd lock the car between trips and still be fearful I'd be ripped off, even though I lived in a very safe, somewhat sterile neighborhood. The metaphor of the maps strikes me: I didn't know where I was, and I didn't know where I was going. It was terrifying, and evoked all of my insecurities.

What was so different about this change? I was *alone.* Traveling as a family, I was often the map reader, a mover of bags and people, a planner. I also frequently took the role of taking care of the kids while my husband bought tickets, planned where to catch planes, trains, buses, etc. I seemed to know what to do and how to behave if I was either responsible for someone else (my kids and husband) or being taken care of by someone else (my husband). And it was true, even in this new situation, that when a daughter or friend arrived in San Francisco, I could be the tour guide, the giver of information, the one to say, "Go call up the bus line and get *them* to tell you how to get there." My ability to be resourceful in helping others was still present, but I couldn't quite do it for myself.

Who am I when I am not depending on anyone and when no one is depending on me? When I am in charge of myself, and only myself, what do I do? Sometimes I panicked.

What a woman's number this is! It is so much easier to tell someone else how to do it—my husband, my boss, my children—than to be faced with the full responsibility myself. How many years and how many times have I given good advice on how to run a meeting, how to teach a class, how to write a book, how to set up the Peace Corps project, as the "power behind the throne"? I have a lot of creative ideas, good notions, important values, yet few of them have been acted upon with me in full charge. The woman's role is to be deprived of that sense of self and *direction*. (Interestingly, that's what maps are for—to get a sense of the direction.) My direction may not be to build a bigger building or develop a bigger organization, but I need my *own* sense of direction.

It is not just being *dependent* that deprives us of our sense of self-direction. It is also being *depended upon* that gives us the excuse not to search and *be* for ourselves. It is easy for me to find the way if someone is depending on me to get there. I've never considered myself a very dependent person; nor do I think others have ever seen me that way. But I do think I have been dependent on others needing me: my children, my husband, and my friends. Although I have no desire to be a hermit, I do wonder how, in such aloneness, one gets a sense of oneself. The issue hidden beneath the maps on the wall, and the unwillingness to go out in the street and *ask* the bus driver how to get there was how to be ultimately responsible for myself.

Loneliness would set in on evenings and weekends. I appreciated the long-distance phone calls from daughters and friends; but the thousands of miles between us accentuated my need to love and be loved.

There were times, during this limbo period (which lasted off and on for at least a year), that I felt anxious, depressed, and lonely. Occasionally I felt an irrational terror. Such fear or panic tends to immobilize me, a frightening thing in itself for such an active person.

Rerooting

How does one put new roots down? Shifting from mother-home-base in the suburbs to living alone in a two-room apartment in a city with my children available mostly by phone was a tremendous adjustment.

Surrendering to the condition that *is*, seems to be the beginning of the process of change. "The surrender is basically a very alone experience. It is analogous to the birth process in which change involves moving from security and protection into another stage which is unknown....One relinquishes oneself to the process, without knowing or worrying about where it will lead, because that is anathema to the process itself."[1]

In my journal I describe some of that surrender:

> Today I have been aware of not allowing myself to *feel* the strangeness, the fear, the insecurity in having to build a new life, make new professional contacts, and build some sort of reputation in this city. I've *known* it would come but hadn't realized it is with me. My somewhat frantic, compulsive past ten days of *not* being centered, have to do with not letting the fear *in*.
>
> I woke up feeling anxious and thought, "Oh, shit, do have to make my own way, *again*?" Can I? Is there such a economic recession that I'll find no pay for my talents and abilities? What do I *really* want to work at now, anyway??? need some structure in my life. Spending full time trying to make myself known professionally here is lonely, and I'm afraid of rejection and failure.

It seems that there were several ways that I kept myself reality-oriented during this time of being rootless, floaty, and spaced out. One was by writing a lot of letters to friends back

[1]Marie Wells summarizes in "Report on the First Conference on Life Transitions," sponsored by The Center for Designed Change, Mill Valley, Ca.

East. I needed to have the bridge still there and to get a sense of my own history and progress (or lack of it) by writing about it. The fact that I kept carbon copies of many letters lends evidence to my need to write for *myself*—to concretize my life—as well as to connect with others.

Another way I kept myself grounded was to be aware of my body, of the physical tensions this transition was causing, and to do something about that stress. There are sentences appearing in many letters during the first six months of my settling that refer to physical pain:

> . . .my gut was literally in screaming pain . . .I think my body is telling me to cool it. . . .I never did let down . . . .I'm feeling run down and achy and don't know how much of it is because I need more rest and how much of it is facing up to the real job of getting known here, of living alone, of earning a living. . .all of it, I guess.
>
> . . .at the moment I'm feeling fragile. With my daughters out of the nest and that life-to-be-created out in front of me, I get shaky inside (which doesn't show much on the outside). I've signed up for two full days a week for a dance workshop, which may help.

Almost instinctively, I found a program that would help me deal with the tension and pain by pursuing physical activity:

> I am in Anna Halprin's dance workshop/training program. How did I float into such total involvement in the thing that is most difficult for me? Some magnet pulled me there to begin with. The joy of being free to move in space feels beautiful. I can integrate my body movement with my feelings and my art work. It also releases some of the pain in my gut, even if only temporarily. Though strenuous and exhausting, it creates a whole new energy in me. Learning how to be uninhibited in movement feels great.

The physical pain would go away during the dance class, but be back with me full strength the next morning. Since the pain did not subside, I wrote a letter to my brother, who is a doctor:

> I thought it would be good for me to write this—for me to admit to *me* and you how often and and how much physical pain I'm in. I have been trying to deal with it myself, alone, in ways that I think are sensible, and avoid, wherever possible taking pills, having to see a doctor, etc. . . . I wake up with a sore stomach . . . I'm eating the right things and not drinking alcohol, but I still hurt a lot. I just drew a picture of how that area inside me feels and it is full of hot reds and black jagged lines. Just looking at the picture scares me!

It helped to share the depth of my pain with him. What did to help *myself* was to spend time putting my feelings on paper, which resulted in much opening up of tears and anger. I put those tears in a picture and came to some sense of self-integration. I also decided to take care of myself by having a superb massage from a woman friend who truly has healing hands. By accepting this part of myself that I really do not like (the stomach that screeches out "you're hurting!" when I think I am sailing along okay), by taking care of my body through dance and massage and rest, and by admitting the pain to some friends, it gradually went away.

My point is that a life change causes a great deal of physical stress. John K. Wood, in an unpublished paper entitled "Living With Life Changes," summarizes many research studies which correlate onset of illness to periods of transition:

> The effects [of change] . . .are often visible in mental anguish and even physical illnesses . . . . The Holmes group, along with Richard Rahe, have studied thousands of persons, and several cultures, and have shown that there is an association between

major life changes in a person's life and the onset of illness.

Many persons emerge from major life transitions stronger, more productive, and more fulfilled than before entering the transition. Too many do not. Many more could. The prospects of making successful transitions might become better if we could learn to understand the nature of change and devise ways to facilitate the process.

Finding my way professionally was an important step in helping me overcome my fears and become grounded. Having built a bridge before coming eased the difficulty of starting anew. Having the beginnings of our center for social change was a base. In a letter, I wrote:

We don't want to do stuff just to earn money, though we need it. We spend a lot of time, at present, just talking, dreaming, sorting out what is most important to us and how we could go about making it happen. The whole male/female revolution is what is personally important to us, as are persons in transition: transition from one country to another, transition into old age, career changes, separations of all natures . . .divorce, widowhood . . .how to plan for and manage personal and organizational change—that is what we are talking about. The three of us are a good support group for each other.

Making new friends was also an important part of my feeling grounded here. The network system works, if slowly. It was a constant effort to look up friends of friends. When I met people I liked, I would follow up by asking to see them again. I realized that every new acquaintance was a potential friend. But *I* had to take the initiative.

Each new situation seemed double-edged: there was the excitement of being me without any history, and the ghastly realization that no one could possibly know me unless I went to great effort to say who I was and what my life had been. Each time I would start with someone new, I would gulp, say to myself, "Here I go again," and launch into what seemed, for that day anyway, the story of my life. It was (and is) a strain to keep this up. For the most part, my pioneering energy was so high that the people-response to me was positive. This fed back into my own energy source.

How people in the network system, or the community, reach out to newcomers can make a big difference to those who are in transition. Again I quote from Wood's paper:

> A sensitive and understanding group of people can provide an environment where one can explore alternatives, gain support, and if necessary fragment, be in crises, and come back together again. It can be a place to dream new dreams. The group offers options, brainstorms, ideas, suggests people to seek out. It is not only a place for moral support but also for realistic suggestions. It is the beginning of a human network and support system which can help one through the various stages of transition and reach into the future.

Building the bridge and having some people here for me was, and is, important. When I first wrote this, I was still beginning the process of putting myself here, for real. Sometimes I would think, "So what's the big deal? Thousands of people move every day! So what?" The "so what" is that transitions are painful, disorienting times when we feel craziness or fear which can cause illness and immobilization. Perhaps we can begin to understand the process of leaving part of ourselves behind, of going into the chaotic no-where land temporarily, of taking careful note of the messages we feel during that time and move to a new selfhood. Perhaps we can help each other through such rites of passage by listening deeply to each other, by participating in the mourning process, and by celebrating the rebirth.

It has been important to me to look at my own life changes as a way of conceptualizing the process of transition. Designing my own change and helping others to do the same

s important to me, both personally and professionally.
Studying my own process, rethinking, reliving, and getting
eedback on it, is a rich learning experience. It is when I tie
ogether the threads of what I have read with my own life
xperience that I have truly learned something. When I have
hus learned, I can use that knowledge and apply it to
1ew situations.

3
Solo
A Midlife Choice

When I was cleaning out my attic preparing to leave the East Coast I found many mementos: a high school diary full of puppy love, college papers written on philosophy and religion, love letters during courtship and marriage, a pack of papers four years old called "divorce negotiations." Among these things I found a notebook I had written at age twenty. The prose that caught my eye was called, "Alone." I was interested then, as I am now, in the difference between being alone and being lonely.

> . . .to be alone for a day, an hour, a night, is to turn thoughts and senses inward; to look and see nothing, but to feel something. To be alone and yet not lonely is one of the greatest joys: To sit by myself with my dreams, vague as they are, is that joy. Aloneness is to *feel*—to be enveloped in feeling; to sense the air, the noise, the smell, and then to sense nothing but sense itself. To be alone is not to be lonely . . . . Aloneness is not pain, it is not tragedy, it is not fear or fear of fear. It is a closeness to the elements—the universe. To have someone at your side to share beauties, is delight. But to observe them alone, knowing that you are not alone in spirit, is to feel the depth, the height, the color of the beautiful emptiness.

Dusting off the mildew from the notebook and reading that statement brought me to the realization that for the first time since I was twenty I would again be alone. It moved me deeply.

I write about what churns inside me—then and now—in order to find peace for myself. Writing is a way of confronting my fears and negative experiences, by plunging into them.

I wrote this chapter three years after settling in California. As I wrote it, I realized that aloneness was not just something that happened to me, something thrust upon me from the outside, but rather an experience which some part of me was seeking, despite the moments of pain attending it. The dialogue with myself helps overcome the loneliness.

And I write to share my thought process with you about the pain, the pleasure and the purpose of living solo. Today the word "solo" conjures up many positive images and meanings for me:

Solo flight: an exciting, risky adventure into the unknown.

Solo performance: to perform alone with or without back-up accompaniment.

Solo: standing on one's own two feet, facing the world.

Solo: alone, as in a cozy cocoon.

Solo, solitary, single, solitude, alone. So/low? Lonely? That is the fear, isn't it?

At a workshop where we were to be known only by fictitious names, names which felt meaningful to us, I chose the name Solo. I liked the sound and the fit of my new name. A few friends still call me Solo. I was surprised that some participants reacted to my name with fear. To them the word meant isolated, separate, unsupported. As I listened to them I understood their fear—the dread of loneliness.

I looked up the word, solo, in the *Thesaurus:* alone, solitary, insular, apart, separated, detached, removed; lone, lonely, lonesome, friendless, homeless, unaccompanied, unaided.

How different from my own imagery! There is scarcely a positive word in that list. No wonder my new name seemed threatening to some people.

In this chapter I am looking at what it means to be a

woman in midlife alone. Three or four years is not a long history of aloneness upon which to draw. However, the sudden experience of singlehood after forty-six years of family life puts some of those feelings into sharp focus. After living a life *with* and *for* people for so long, my need to find the direction and meaning of life for myself was tremendous. Although my initial imagery is positive and exciting, underneath it lies the possibility of being isolated, lonesome, and unsupported.

Loneliness, What Is It?

Loneliness is seldom listed in the index of any psychology text. My hunch is that it is such a devastating experience that even the psychologists have overlooked it. Anger, anxiety, fear, trust, rejection are all listed. But loneliness—that emotion which seems to keep people on a frantic treadmill to avoid it—is not dealt with. It is poets, novelists, and songwriters who voice the pain of loneliness.

When I think of a lonely person, two pictures come to mind. One is a woman sitting huddled on a cold grey slab (a grave?), head bent, knees clasped to chest. It is a drizzly day. She is in excruciating pain. There are no people in sight. A deathly silence encloses the scene. The other image is that of a graceful figure standing with face uplifted, reaching out with every muscle only to find empty, blank faces and people with their backs turned.

These two images describe for me the two forms of loneliness: 1) separation and loss: death, tragedy, uprootedness, divorce, rejection, separation from loved ones, abandonment; 2) being ignored or misunderstood by important others, being listened to but not *heard*, feeling misunderstood, misinterpreted, having knowledge or experience that no one else seems to understand, feeling alone in a crowd, or not connecting in a relationship.

The first form of loneliness, caused by loss, is written about a great deal, and each of us has experienced it in some

form. My losses—divorce, uprooting myself, and the separation from my daughters—have brought me face to face with
that kind of loneliness.

The second form of loneliness, not being heard, is less
often described. It is this category of loneliness I wish
to discuss.

Carl Jung puts it this way in *Memories, Dreams, Reflections:*
"Loneliness does not come from having no people about one,
but from being unable to communicate the things that seem
important to oneself."

Woman's Loneliness

This rings true for me. Some of my loneliest feelings have
to do with being a woman desperately wanting and speaking
out for the equality of women, and when I speak out, finding
either no response or misunderstanding. For example, I was
giving a brief talk as a panelist at the American Psychological
Association and voiced the idea that our summer workshop
staff was a model of sexual equality. My voice was animated as
I spoke, and I looked to the audience expecting an echo of my

excitement. There was no response, no ripple of enthusiasm in the audience. Then a male panelist stood up and joked and charmed the audience's attention away from the issues into a mood of entertainment. I alone was not entertained; anger was mixed with loneliness as I found myself unsupported in my pursuit of issues and one-upped by a man.

For women, perhaps loneliness and loving a man are intertwined in this stage of our cultural development. In California, I found myself loving a man who had little understanding of the oppression of women. He has been raised in the old tradition. He would say, regarding my work to help women find their stengths, assertiveness and power: "You have the right to pursue your efforts for equality, but I don't understand it all." His attitude left me feeling lonely in a very important part of our relationship. I would prefer a partner who shared my emotional and intellectual understanding of the cause and effect of the oppression of women. It would be fantastic if he were there cheering me on. It is a rare male who has liberated himself in that way, however. And, of course, the choice to love this man is mine.

My women friends who are in constructive, loving partnerships with men say they need the companionship, support, nurturance and understanding of women. For those of us trying to channel human energy into opportunities for women there is no substitute for enlightened female friends. Without them, deep loneliness sets in.

Carl Rogers says a person is most lonely when he has dropped something of his outer shell or facade, the face with which he has been meeting the world, and feels sure that no one can understand, accept, or care for the portion of his inner self that lies revealed.

He is describing a time when one feels extremely vulnerable and *potentially* lonely. How that vulnerability is dealt with by the people nearby determines whether that person will feel lonely. If I peel off my facade and the important figures close to me do not understand or care for me as this more open, raw individual, then I feel extremely lonely. Perhaps I will put the mask back on. On the other hand, if people listen to me and appreciate me for the open qualities I have just revealed, then my exposure will feel worthwhile. I can begin to develop the new self beneath the facade.

Rogers continues with the notion that when this mask is dropped the individual may feel: "If anyone comes to know me as I *really* am inside, he could not possibly respect or love me!" This is when our awareness of being lonely is keenest. It is a time of profound personal risk.

Clark Moustakas is one of the few writers who has put poetry and psychology together in his beautiful work, *Loneliness and Love.* He says: "Paul Tillich believed that two words were created in the English language to express the two sides of man's aloneness—'loneliness' to express pain in being alone and 'solitude' to express the glory of being alone. As Tillich saw it, loneliness is most widespread when we are left alone through separation or death, but it also occurs in those moments when the person feels absolutely isolated or misunderstood or when he remains silent and withdrawn though surrounded by people he loves. There is also the loneliness of disapppointed love or rejected love; and finally there is the loneliness of guilt (the failure to be one's real self) and the loneliness of having to die, of anticipating death in the actual day or hour of our dying."

Moustakas believes that everyone needs to experience the pain of loneliness to become reacquainted with himself—to know the glory of being himself and setting up an honest, personal value system. "Being lonely is a desolate, critical state...but being lonely can bring you in touch with yourself."

Losing one's *identity* is a profoundly lonely experience. I have described how I lost my sense of self through blindly following society's sex role expectations. "The greatest danger, that of losing one's own self, may pass off quietly as if it were nothing; every other loss, that of an arm or a leg, five dollars, etc. is sure to be noticed."[1] This is an example of being

---

[1] Soren Kierkegaard, quoted by Carl Rogers in *Becoming Partners, Marriage and Its Alternatives,* New York: Delacorte Press, 1972. p.15

lonely *within* a relationship. It is a form of loneliness familiar to many American women as they are isolated in suburban houses serving families eighteen hours a day. Women's loneliness can develop amidst very busy, people-oriented days. My own loneliness within marriage was an important turning point. Out of that well of despair I began to re-form myself, my priorities, and my values.

Being lonely, for me, has very little to do with being *alone*. It has to do with not having an identity, not knowing who or what I am, not having an inner core or center. If I have that identity or inner core, then times of being alone become times of creativity and self-expression, of peaceful meditation, or connecting with the persons I love spiritually, or by writing or telephoning them.

Being lonely for me is also being out of touch; not being touched physically, and being out of touch with myself. The notion that these two things are connected came to me in my new California setting where body massage is an acceptable form of non-sexual pleasure. While taking in the soothing strokes I concentrated on my physical self: my breathing, my tensions, aches, and pains. I listened to what my body was telling me. Getting a massage doesn't take the place of a close, physical, loving relationship, but it helps me experience my body as a source of pleasure and of self-knowledge.

Being lonely is connected to an inability to love. If I dislike myself, then time alone becomes a spiral of self-hatred. There is no positive energy in me for exploring myself—my ideas, creative notions, or fun. If I can love myself and be connected to the persons I love—even in their absence—I can feel peace. Of course, I miss people when they are not with me, but the horrible, clawing loneliness is not part of their absence if I write to, or let the essence of that person into my heart and feel the love between us.

The loneliness I spoke of during my first six months of rerooting was closely connected with not knowing who I was. Who am I when I am not defined: by a husband; by children; by professional links?

Even my goals and directions for work were shifting, and

by trying to create my own job I didn't even have an acceptable professional label. And I was no longer "the wife of _____." When meeting new people I wondered how I would tell them about myself. I think I had spent most of my conversational hours during my marriage talking about what my husband and children were doing. I distinctly remember the first time I said, "I'd rather not talk about what my husband is doing, I'd like to tell you about myself."

"Who am I when my children are not there to need me?" At first there was no answer. I looked into myself and found loss, desolation, emptiness. I fantasized having another baby who would be dependent on me and whom I could nurture. Rather than create another person I needed to re-create myself!

The Vision Quest

It must have been an intuitive sense of my need to re-create myself through an exploration of solitude that sent me on the Vision Quest trip. It was an instinctive, spontaneous leap into the frightening unknown. It was a way of exploring the boundaries of my aloneness, an acknowledgement that as a middle-aged woman my next journey was to be inner and spiritual.

The following is from my journal:

Death Valley: Day one of my solo: Wednesday
To grasp it, the reality-unreality of it, I need to write. I am fortunate in that I am out of the cold wind, in a spot not far from our clan base camp. There are no trees or large bushes on the whole horizon. What faces me is a bare mountain, stone, sagebrush, and craggy rocks jetting upward. My god! What *am* I doing here, alone for three days to come, with only water? (and honey, tea, and boullion). I've never slept outside alone anywhere and here I am in the middle of the most barren of places for three days alone without food. I'm not quite sure why I'm doing this. It has been a mixture of camaradarie, fun and misery, so far. It is a challenge!

Two months ago I walked into an agency, Rites of Passage,[2] to say hello to a few colleagues. Stephen,[2] an acquaintance, was writing lists and drawing up charts. "Whatcha doin?" I asked. With excited eyes he started to unfold his interest in the American Indian. He was planning one of his survival trips with adolescents and adults to learn respect for nature and oneself.

Before I had walked out I had signed myself up for a seven-day trip to Death Valley. We would spend five days on the desert, three of which would be a "solo-fast." We would learn the ways of the Indians and the meaning of questing for a vision.

Time? Since writing the first pages, I've slept. Before going to sleep in the high sun I wanted some notion of how long I had slept on awakening, so I put a little stick up and marked where the shadow was. When I awoke, the shadow had moved an inch. So, I've slept in the sun "one inch." How long is that, I wonder?

I sure am tired. I was tired before these seven days began. The previous weeks have been jammed with meetings and teaching classes. After having dinner guests on Sunday Frances (my daughter) showed me how to roll my clothes tightly for my back pack. Her experienced hands adjusted the straps to my shoulders. She attempted to allay my fears. The role-reversal was amusing and heartwarming as she helped "pack up Mom for camp." As she drove me to the clan gathering place at 11 p.m. her fond farewell was "Take care and have fun!" We both laughed at the turn-about.

Time dragged between 11 p.m. and 4 a.m. as we gathered together to leave. The nurse talked and re-hashed the "what to do if you get bitten by a snake." I listened and I didn't listen. I wanted to know what to do and I didn't want to face that possibility as a reality. At 4 a.m., we got . . .

At this minute, as I am sitting in total wilderness, I hear a tremendous earth shaking booom! Fortunately I had read the sign as we crossed Death Valley. It said "Experimental area for test flights. Sonic Booms." So at least I know what it is. But how ironic. Jets moving down that empty valley faster than sound and me without a human around, in a little cave

[2]For information regarding scheduled trips, write Stephen and Meridith Foster, Rites of Passage, 857 DeLong Ave., Novato, CA 94947

without food (and I'm beginning to get hungry). The contrast is almost too much.

To go back to our departure: we packed the van, the trucks and a little VW. I claimed a comfortable spot in the van next to Stephen who was driving. At first that seemed selfish, then it seemed okay. The initial flash of energy betweeen us, two months ago, was what started me on this venture. I wanted to get to know this intense person. At 4 a.m. having no sleep, we started out, caravan style; ten people in the van— eight high school kids and Stephen and me . . .

God, it feels good to be warm and out of the wind. I had prepared myself for heat but not for cold weather. We were soooo cold the last two nights! Wonder how I'll keep warm tonight? The sun is going down behind my mountain fairly fast. While it's still warm I'll venture forth to pee and to gather wood for a fire tonight and to get some exercise. It would be easy to just sit here the rest of the day keeping warm in my sleeping bag . . . .

Sobering, very sobering. As I walked away from my warm cave-like shelter, I was stepping lightly feeling carefree. Suddenly I froze stiff as I saw before me a coiled snake, black tail upward, body rigid, waiting to strike. It was about sixteen inches long, sandy colored; exactly the color of the pink-brown earth. It had dark stripes and a small triangular head. It looked more like what I remember as a copperhead than a rattlesnake. Its black tail did not appear to have rattles on it, but then I was paralyzed with fright. I'm not sure what I saw. I stared: it was powerful, poised, ready to strike. Apparently it had heard me coming. Damn lucky I was looking where I was going! I moved uphill and it slid sideways, slinking down the slope. Returning after my pee, I took a slightly different route.

Now what do I do? I was beginning to feel good about these three days alone. Now I am sobered. Real emergencies are possible! I am wondering if anyone could really hear this dumb little whistle or if my buddy Emily could possibly *see* a red bandana if I used it as an emergency signal. I doubt it. I realize I don't know enough about how to treat myself if bitten. How can Stephen be in this desert for weeks at a time and never see a single snake and I have this happen to me on my first day alone? When I picked this spot, I said to myself, "If I were a snake, I'd choose this ledge." Damn! My question is whether to stay here tonight and try to cooexist with the snake

or whether to move down to the clan camp site where it i
much windier and colder. I'll decide later. For now I'm toasty

It is very, very quiet and still, except for the wind. Two
birds perched nearby earlier. They were a welcome surprise
There is so little life around. Why does the only active life have
to be a poisonous snake? I'd better take another look at tha
snakebite kit and really read the instructions.

My head aches, so I take a salt tablet and some more
water. I think I keep writing in order to be *doing* something. *I'm
not quite willing, yet, to do nothing in my aloneness.*

Now I'm sitting by my little fire making myself some tea
before I crawl in to keep warm. The smartest thing I did was to
wear thermal underwear and bring a pair of warm gloves
Trying to write with them on is a bit difficult.

I wandered around this afternoon in my canyon (or wash
as it's called) and made the beginnings of my ceremonial space
for the vision quest. It was a careful, thoughtful ritual, jus
preparing the place. I searched for a large, flat space in the
canyon, I built an attractive centerpiece out of stones and a
dried shrub and flower. The centerpiece is supposed to have a
live bush, but I choose to arrange the center with shapes tha
were meaningful to me. Then I proceeded to arrange the space
as we had been told the Sioux Indians do. Ten paces from th
center toward the west I placed a pole (in my case all I coul
find were small dried bush branches, but I chose them care
fully for their attractiveness). Then I made a path back to th
centerpoint. Ten paces to the north, I placed another pole
then back to the center. Then to the east, then south. As I wa
doing this, all slowly and carefully, I was thinking about how
was going to place my power objects on the poles and do th
ritual itself on the third day of my solo. When I finished placin
the poles at all four compass points I decided to connect then
into a circle. I wanted to adjust the Indian ritual to my own
needs. It felt right to encompass those four poles with a circle
making a mandala ceremonial space. So I made a round path
touching each pole.

I am not looking forward to tonight! I am cold and scared.

Moontime. 9 or 10 p.m.? How can I possibly sleep? It is s
beautiful and exciting here. I'm snuggled in against the cliff i
my high-up perch. I watched the mountains in the far distanc
turn soft-edged grey-pink. Dusk was soothing. I wondered

I'd be frightened, but instead am awe-struck. The stars appeared slowly and I was trying to recognize the constellations when I realized that behind me was a very bright light. I turned to see the full moon appear over the deep black evening mountain. Now my side of the valley is clear and bright by the light of the moon. The hill opposite me is in the contrasting dark shadow. The wind has died down, but it is still damn cold. I've lit my candle to write this but I can read it by the moonlight.

I am a moon-child these days. I get great energy from the full moon. When it appeared I felt at home . . . .I'll stop writing and turn my attention to the moon.

Day 2 of Solo: Thursday, sunrise
As I wait for the sun to actually appear over the mountain behind me, I see the bright light on the mountains ahead and the valley below. A snow capped peak is in the far distance due south. Its angular shape is dramatized by the early sun rays and deep shadows.

Listening to the silence is a powerful and profound experience. At first I avoided listening. Silence is so totally foreign it is frightening to allow myself to become aware of it. I can sit quietly now for a half hour awaiting the sunrise and—now that the wind is quiet—hear total nothingness except for my own breathing and the rustle of my movements, however slight. I can see the valley and the mammoth range about twenty miles away, but I can hear nothing but a slight, constant ringing. I think it is my own inner ear. Is that possible? There are no crickets, no birds, no trees that bend in the wind, no human sounds—nothing! I will try to soak in that silence more completely later. I fear letting go of myself into that total quiet, yet that's what I want to do. I sang last night as the sun set, partly to hear my own sound.

Events of last night: After watching the moon mount, I crawled more completely into my sleeping bag with my head pulled in. The drawstring on the bag doesn't close tightly, so I placed the top of my head (hat on) into the remaining hole to seal me in more completely. I was dreaming I was in the middle of the desert valley—the totally sandy barren part of Death Valley—and I was in a phone booth! The phone rang, and when I answered it, I said, "Hello, this is the wilderness!"...(I laugh now thinking of it)...then I suddenly awoke knowing that something was moving on my head and hat. My hands started to jump towards my head to find out what it was, but fortunately the sleeping bag was constricting my movement, and I wakened enough to *think*. "Be quiet hold still, listen!" My heart was pounding, adrenalin shot through my system. I was hot for a change! "This is one way to get warm," I say to myself. As I stayed motionless I felt the movement on my head again. It seemed like a scratching sort of movement. My fear was that it was my friend the snake trying to join me in my sleeping bag to keep warm. Hearing such stories around the campfire two nights ago had been a good education, but now I was terrified. So I waited in silence. I couldn't tell if the rustle I heard was my own breathing jostling the sleeping bag, or whether it was a snake slithering around me or under me, or on top of me. My reason told me it was a rodent trying to get into the plastic bag medical kit which was stashed in a little ledge in my nook. I wiggled a bit to see if that would stir a reaction. It didn't seem to. After about ten minutes of wondering, listening, and moving slightly now and then, my panic subsided. I decided to push the top of my head out of the drawstring hole. (To do so earlier might have invited the creature to come in.) I peered out. I could see clearly, in the moonlight, but did not see any animal. I pulled myself to a sitting position, still in the bag, to take a look around, being careful to move slowly. I saw nothing. Finding my little flashlight I beamed it around wondering if it had all been my imagination. I went back to sleep only to be awakened again by the exact same thing two more times. By then I had figured out it was a rodent. The scratching on my cap was so definitely a paw. It was obviously not a large creature or it would have made more noise moving. Figuring it wouldn't do much damage to let a rat investigate my hat (thank god for the hat), I went to sleep. The relief that it was not the snake made rodent seem friendly.

This morning, before writing (and I haven't gotten out of bed yet) I examined my immediate surroundings for clues of my visitor. At first I saw only one small turd on the little shelf with my flashlight. A small rat, I say to myself. Then saw six or seven larger turds tucked in the little area where I have propped up my candle. These are closer to an inch in size and have white on them. Ordinarily I don't give a shit (good pun) what size or shape some turd is, but at this moment it matters to me. What animal did it? Why does that animal like my little candle holder space? And why is it attracted to my wool hat? And most importantly, where does it go when it's not here? And will it bite me? It can stay as long as I can stay peacefully, too.

.... The sun is bright. I am at last getting really warm. Looks like a beautiful day. I am glad I am alone, here. I don't want to share this day with someone. I want it by myself. That is new, for me! I'm not particularly hungry now, though my stomach hurt a little when I awoke. My luxury was to brush my teeth before getting out of bed. Water, medical kit, writing paper, drawing materials, candle, and flashlight are ordered on a ledge next to me: my very own nest. Today I'd like to draw and take pictures and meditate. Survival won't take up so much time if the weather stays lovely.

.... High noon. It's colder today than I predicted. The wind coming down the wash is cold, so I haven't ventured more than a hundred yards. Why bother, I like it here, and there is nothing I *have* to do. Fantastic! I've drawn one picture of the moon-scene last night, fixed the moleskin on my feet to protect them from the blisters I was getting, and just took a short nude sunbath until the cold wind came sneaking into my space. I put Wylers lemonade into some of my drinking water and have polished off a quart already. I'm not hungry, which amazes me, but I am very thirsty.

Day 2: about 6 p.m.

Tonight I worried about the others. It's very cold and the sun hasn't even gone down yet. The wind blows fiercely every few minutes. I've never heard wind the way I hear it in this place. I can tell when it is about a mile away getting whipped up to push through this canyon. The noise gets louder and louder; then, woosh, it comes galloping through and disappears. Then it is quiet until the same routine starts once more.

I hope Emily is okay on top of my mountain. Did she find a sheltered spot up there? I keep looking up to see if I can see her red bandana as a signal. I'm afraid I would not be able to see it even if she did put it up. When I watched her climb up there she appeared to be a small dark figure in the distance. It was enough to just pick out the human form at the top, I'd never see a bandana!

Stephen, are you shivered to the bone? You hate the cold. You didn't have enough warm clothes. You have a fantastic sleeping bag, though. And Vicky? And Lisa? Did you decide to stay together in Lisa's cave?

This morning as the sun was beginning to shine, snow flakes fell. Who knew we were going to fight cold instead of heat in Death Valley at Easter time? Please don't die, anyone!

I am thinking about the morning we hiked to base camp. We put on our packs and started the short but difficult (for me) hike west. I learned a little humility. I always like to be one of the best in everything I do, and with thirty-five pounds on my back and no experience carrying it, I realized I just did not have good stamina. I envy that kind of stamina—not brute strength, but stamina—and have never had a lot though I have always been athletic. Even though I've been walking the hills of San Francisco, I still had to stop often to let the pain in my chest subside. I could see our destination and realized it really wasn't very far. I questioned whether I could make it. Then figured, of course I could make it if I took one step at a time and took as long as I wanted. I took the pressure off myself to keep up with the others. "I can be last and still be an okay person," I tried to convince myself. There was one girl behind me who was having more difficulty than I. I could try to help her keep her courage up. She was crying, "I can't do it!" The whole metaphor of life in our culture hit me: competition, envy; trying to be one of the best in whatever we do; feeling some comfort if there is someone less able than ourselves, helping that person as a way of helping ourselves.

I did make it, and was exhausted. Slept hard on the hard ground that night. After getting up and having breakfast, we packed the remaining food in big plastic bags and buried it until our return. We were about to venture on our solo days which included fasting. We filled our gallon water bottles at the spring. That is, if you can call an eight-inch hole a spring. When I first came wandering to look for this noted desert spring I was dumbfounded to find midst the white, dry, tall reeds a small hole that was filled with water. It looked as though there might be one quart of water in it, total. This was no bubbling, clean mountain brook! I wondered, as I looked at it, how thirty people could possibly get two or three gallons of water each out of this mucky looking spot. Yet, the value, of that little spot, was of great import. Slowly, with my meta-cup, I "spooned" the water into the jugs. Again, a metaphor for life: one small spring as the source of life for many beings.

Day 3: Solo
Sunrise. I slept okay. No visit from my rodent friend. I was so restless, I tossed around to find a place of comfort for my aching sore body. Perhaps this kept the creature away. Now I am waiting for the sun to push itself up over the mountain again. Maybe today I will clear a spot and have a fire near me for the night. That would be a nice change. How do the others manage without gloves? I couldn't write this without them.

The wind eventually calmed down last night as the stars came out. I just watched, bundled up, and waited for the moon. Again, it was a sight full of drama and music. The sky lightens outlining the massive mountain which becomes velvet black in shadow. Lighter and brighter come the edges and then the moon appears—luminous and clear. It rises steadily changing the shadows on the mountains thirty miles away. I heard most of a symphony while I watched.

Today is the last day of solo. I wish it were over tonight. Maybe getting a fire ready will help. I'm still worried about the kids. Some of them don't seem to use their heads to survive.

I remember two dreams of last night. In the first one I was looking for the animal that disturbed me. I looked in my kitchen oven (with a glass window in it). The oven was turned on. I saw a panda bear looking out at me with soulful eyes. It was really cute. "Oh, I'm sorry," I said, "I didn't want to hurt you. I just wanted to know who you were!" I felt badly that I was roasting the panda. My associations: Bear: I am a bear in the clan on this solo. Oven: I'm cold and need warmth. Maybe the dream is me, the bear, trying to keep warm in the oven, trying to discover who I am. Could be.

The other dream. I had bought an old house for us to live in. I was still married, and the girls were little. It was bedtime. I had run the garbage disposal and gone down to the basement to turn on an old washing machine. When I did, tremendous floods of water and garbage started vomiting out of the disposal—just pumping away red blood and brown gook! My husband stood and just watched and kept saying, "It's the food you put down there this morning!" I felt responsible, misunderstood, angry. He was useless and unhelpful. We went to the bedroom where the wallpaper was flowered and old and peeling. The window frames were rotten. I began to cry. "I don't want to spend our weekends fixing up this mess do you?" "No," he said, "Why don't you see if you can find a student to help you out and I'll pay for it." That dream left me with such a heavy feeling I don't want to think about it now. Later, maybe.

Come on, *sun!* Make it over the mountain! I'm cold and want to get out and pee! My ass is sore from sitting!

*   *   *

What am I learning out here, anyway? That I have tremendous inner strength and resources if left to myself. That I don't get lonely when alone. I've been discovering that about myself for a year, now. At age forty-six, for the first time in my whole life, I've been living alone in San Francisco. I've always lived with people: before I was married I had roommates, then marriage for twenty years...divorce...followed by one daughter living with me all the time. Living alone and being lonely are two entirely different things! I was often more lonely in the marriage.

I am discovering that if I have a pen and drawing material with me, I don't need much more.

I'm learning that I care enough for myself to take care of myself. That seems foolishly simple.

I am learning, somehow, about death. Although I have tremendous energy and excitement about living, the idea of dying does not frighten me. I envision death as becoming one with the cosmos. I find myself self-protective, but less out of death-fear than out of life-wish.

I've changed a lot in the past three years. Three summers ago I remember driving from Santa Cruz to San Francisco. (I was in California for a summer visit.) I was alone. I got very spooked when I parked the car to get out and walk on the beach alone. I had to climb down a cliff to get to the shore. My fantasy was that I'd fall and no one would find me until long after I was dead. That was a very lonely feeling. This desert trip was a challenge to overcome those kinds of fears.

So, being alone is not as bad as I had thought, particularly when I know it has an end. I've wondered about true hermits' aloneness with no end. I wonder if they have dialogues with themselves most of the time or if, eventually, the inner dialogue stops and they just exist.

Carlos Castaneda says, "To change our idea of the world is the very crux of sorcery. And stopping the internal dialogue is the only way to accomplish this." I have been trying to turn off my internal dialogue. And that has happened here. Writing this journal helps me get my internal dialogue out, then I can leave the thoughts behind and just be. Doing nothing is not just the absence of doing all the everyday things; it has its own paradoxical completeness. I've written a poem about it.

DEATH VALLEY SOLO

Stark, dry soil.
  Parched white leaves.
    Ghostly
Brittle, contorted twigs
  Grey with age
    Lifeless
Sharp, strong thorns
  Protecting simplest growth
    Biting
Desolate barren desert
  You mock me!
Your moods are swift-shifting,
  Fickle.
I layer myself for warmth—
  The sun pours molten rays.
I awaken to warm sun—
  It snows.
Lonely cold desert
  I am trying to woo you!
    Be my friend . . .

        Silence.   Forever silence

Only wind as it gushes forth
  tumbling fragile bony weeds.

                    Solitary desert,
                        I mock you!
                    I reach inward,
                        finding courage to BE
                        alone,
                            silent,
                            me.

                    I am everything.
                    I am no/thing.

                    *   *   *

   Now I'm getting wiser. I cleared a spot in front of my nook
and built a fireplace and heated some water. Drank a double
dose of hot boullion. Far out! I had been afraid of a brush fire
and unwilling to pull up the bushes to meet my needs. This
morning I was willing to give them a tug. I said, "I'm sorry, it's
you or me," to the bush. (That seems overly dramatic.) I saw
heaps of the turd under the bush. I'm right in thinking a rodent
lives nearby.
   Shall I do the Vision Quest ritual this afternoon? I think
so . . . . Glad I set up the poles and the path on my first solo day.
Don't think I'd bother today. I will change the words of the
prayer or lament, from: "Great Father Spirit have mercy on me
so my people may live." to: "Oh mighty spirit of the universe,
love me so that I may love all people." My version seems less
chauvinistic and clannish and more appropriate to me . . . .

Day 3: Solo, afternoon
   I did the Vision Quest Ritual for about three hours. (I'm
less able to judge time, today, I think, but the sun moved
across the sky and behind the hill.) I quit when I got cold.
   To the West I place three crystal beads tied in red fabric.
The beads are from my father. He bought them in China as
a student.
   To the North I placed a silver pin, tied in red fabric. It
belonged to my mother. I have worn it often.
   To the East I placed a wooden yin/yang earring carved by
my brother for me.
   To the South I placed two objects: one symbolizing me,
one symbolizing my children. The porcelain rose pin is

mine . . .I wore it for years. The African trading bead is from my daughters.

As I walked from the center position to each point on the compass, I moved slowly, with my eyes down, not focusing on anything. I concentrated on my breathing, breathing deeply with each slow step. When I reached the pole with the power object I stood with my head raised to the sky and sang out my chant, loud and clear. It felt good inside to give full strength to my voice. It also surfaced strong emotions. I thought of my family, each in a different setting. I appreciated them fully, without reservations, lovingly. When I stood in front of the objects on the south pole I wept for love of my daughters. Being a mother of such fine persons is a great joy, forever, for me.

I thought of many other people I love. And I didn't think of anything. I lay down within my circle, for a time, I don't know how long. I was calm. Then I started moving around the ritual path again. When I became very cold, I said goodbye to each power object, placing it in the centerpiece for the night. I left the circle quietly.

*   *   *

My last night of solo. It has been a good day, after all.

I surely smell ripe! Have had the same clothes on day and night for six days. I haven't dared use water to wash with except to dab at my face and hands. Water is too precious. I haven't seen my hair. I've had it tied up under my ski cap day and night. I'll welcome a bath and shampoo. I think I'll be glad to see people, too.

My diary stops here. Back in the world I became too busy to put down the feelings of the day. I remember some warm feelings of reunion with the clan and then the whole tribe. Finally the sun gave us a break and warmed our bodies for our last afternoon united. We found ourselves sitting close together talking rapidly of all our experiences, good and bad. The close calls, the danger, the cold and loneliness, the good feelings and the treasures found, the poems written, things that had been hand-crafted. At the dinner fire and first meal together, we stood chanting, singing, clapping and gradually gave our power objects to people we cared for. The giving and receiving was warmly loving, meaningful.

We were cheerful packing up, and the hike out was light and easy. I was in better physical shape than when we had arrived. My feet seemed to move across the rocky ground in the dark with ease. The moon was out again as we drove north on the eastern side of the Sierras. White, snowcapped mountains illuminated by the moon accompanied our pathway home.

We turned off the road at a hot springs around midnight. The scene was like that of a Chinese scroll. Below us was a wide, quickly flowing hot stream. We took the windy path down the hill, hearing the gurgling and bubbling as we walked. The backdrop was high mountains in the disance with the moon watching over us. An arched bridge crossed the stream. Slowly, one by one, we undressed and slipped into the delicious water . . . our first in a week. Thirty beautiful persons bathed in the warmth, the moonlight, the friendship. The stream from the river cast an unearthly air around us. Laughing and playing, quietly rejuvenating, I declared it was the most lovely Easter morning I'd ever seen.

Some Gleanings

I've quoted at length from this journey for several reasons, one of which is that it was an entirely new kind of experience for me, and I'd like to encourage others — particularly women — to be their adventurous selves, no matter what age. I gain courage from seeing other middle-aged women embarking on new lives with high spirit. So I would like you to experience that part of me.

Also, I was enacting the many positive images I have of being solo:

This was a solo flight, for me. It *was* a risky adventure into the unknown. Now that it is past, it doesn't seem so risky or adventurous but at the time it certainly did. I keep learning

hat each new step fills me with uncertainty and anxiety. Once
he step is taken I wonder why I was so fearful.

This was a solo of standing on my own two feet facing the
world. I learned about my own inner resources and strengths.
found life can be interesting for me by myself because I have a
desire to explore, learn, and create. I was just beginning to
discover what I would do with a lot of time alone. One idea for
a future adventure is to spend several weeks alone somewhere, without a phone or visitors. I wonder what that would
be like.

This was a solo as in a cozy cocoon. I felt safe by myself.

This trip was also an unconscious step to find out more
about who I am when I am alone—without any children, and
without a partner. (It interests me that during my three-day
solo I had my first dream in which my ex-husband was identi-
fiable since my divorce four years earlier. It would make sense
hat after twenty years of marriage one would dream about a
former partner. But in my efforts to separate and detach I had
even blocked my unconscious.)

Alone: A Choice

Clark Moustakas puts it well:
"The moment of solitude is a spontaneous awakening, a coming to life in one's own way, a path to authenticity and self renewal."

"Solitude is a return to one's self when the world has grown cold and meaningless, when life has become filled with people and too much of a response to others."

I experienced this kind of solitude, briefly, as I let myself into the silence, the no-thing-ness, the nothingness of the desert. Those intensely quiet, solitary moments were terrifyingly beautiful. I allowed myself to dip into that space and come out of it feeling refreshed and clean. My aloneness was not lonely. From it I learned to value myself. I also learned to make choices, to create the life I wanted to live.

I was beginning to think about *choosing* to be alone or unpartnered. I had escaped from a situation that was hurtful to me—a marriage—thus leaving a void, an emptiness I hadn't chosen to be *alone*. I had chosen to be out of a relationship!

This may seem like a subtle, unimportant difference. But for women who have been married, or programmed that they are incomplete without a man (which most of us are), it takes exploration and relearning to gain a new identity.

I realized that at some point I needed to be honest with myself. Am I living alone because I can't find anyone compatible to live with? Or am I living alone because I prefer it? I am aware that each lifestyle has its own set of problems, but making this second possibility—living solo—a *conscious choice*, is important.

Those of us who are divorced or widowed are faced with these losses and with the added societal standard that women are not attractive after age thirty. (I've even heard twenty-five-year-olds bemoan their loss of sex appeal due to old age. What men and the media are doing to us is outrageous!) If we have had some professional or career training, we are fortunate indeed.

In this new aloneness we have the opportunity for a whole new era of twenty to thirty-five years! If the first twenty years are devoted to growing up and the second twenty to raising a family, there are still two spans of twenty years left to go. No one ever told us to look past age forty-five or fifty. For some women this period means "life is over"; others of us feel life is just beginning. I don't know what determines the path for each woman. I can only describe what is important for me.

In the transition from nurturer of others to nurturer of myself, I asked myself, "What will make it flavorful?" Flavor in life includes the spice! In choosing to live alone the feisty part of me emerges: "Who the hell do they think they are, programming women for 'planned obsolescence'?"

"Middle age is when the image of the future catches up with reality and many women are confronted with their nothingness. At this point in the life cycle the inadequacy of the traditional female roles is apparent. Because not only is this a difficult society in which to be female, it is also a difficult society in which to grow old . . . . In *Sisterhood Is Powerful,* Zoe Moss says 'Everything she reads, every comic strip, every song, every cartoon, every advertisement, man may mature, but women just obsolesce.'"[3]

As I read, watch a smattering of TV and observe how the media portray middle-aged women, I get so angry I am determined to live a life which laughs at those put-downs and show the world what midlife can really be. (Did you ever look at the ads in a medical journal? It shows one depressed middle-aged woman after another needing to be "elevated" with a tranquilizer!) Again, a pinch of anger spices up the pot for me and gives me some zest for speaking out.

Recently I have begun to feel great pride in my age. One very moving experience happened in a dance training program with Anna Halprin. The women and men had separated for the day to explore their own identity through movement. As a theme, the women had chosen the ocean with its

Pauline Bart, "Middle Age: Planned Obsolescence" in *Women and Men: Roles, Attitudes and Power Relationships.* Edited by Eleanor Zuckerman. Published by The Radcliffe Club of New York, Inc., 27 W. 44th St., N.Y., N.Y.).

powerful mystery and rhythm as the symbol of our dance. As we lined ourselves on the beach for a ritual walk to the sea, Anna suggested we proceed in order of age (the oldest leading the way), giving respect to those of many years, acknowledging the importance of experience. As we slowly moved in unison toward the ocean, I felt—for the first time—the great dignity that can come with age if it is felt *within* and acknowledged by others. Those cultures that equate age with wisdom suddenly made great sense to me.

I am also learning to take myself seriously (as well as to laugh and have angry times). It may seem peculiar to think it is necessary to take oneself seriously, but that is exactly what mean. My general attitude in life has been that my ideas or thoughts couldn't really count. It was those others, particularly men, who knew what was going on and had answers. I need to recognize that my ideas, my dreams, my energy, and my abilities do count if I take the time to develop and communicate them.

Sometimes I think I am too serious, but that is quite different from taking *myself* seriously. I've always taken life seriously. But me? Again, it has to do with being a woman. After I've given a talk or made some important point at a committee meeting, it does not thrill me to have someone come up and tell me, "You *looked* stunning!" "Maybe so," say I, "but what did you think about what I *said*?" It is that general attitude that women are meant to look attractive while men are meant to think that makes it difficult for women to be taken seriously. (Did you ever go up to a man after a talk and tell him he *looked* handsome without commenting on the speech?)

Annie Gottlieb speaks of woman's inability to take herself seriously in her introduction to the eloquent book of photographs, *Women See Women:* "And finally there was the persistent problem of inequality in work opportunities and pay, which made it even more difficult for a woman photographer to support herself than a man. But material obstacles and social resistance are the lot of any aspirant of the arts; what has hampered women far more insidiously than any external circumstances is their *ingrained and constantly reinforced lack of conviction that what they do is important.''* (Italics mine.)

Choosing to live solo means the freedom to do all of those things I've always said I wanted to do. That, in itself is frightening. Do I really mean what I've always said? Do I really want to develop my interests in movement and dance? (It has been another confrontation with my internal boundaries to get involved with movement in my mid-forties. I'm always the oldest but feel my energy is very exciting to those around me.) Do I want to explore more of my interests in photography and painting? Will I ever get up enough nerve to travel alone? Is my writing a serious commitment? How will I integrate all of these interests into my profession as a psychotherapist?

Being solo means not hiding behind anyone anymore. There are no excuses left not to do what I want to do. I have only myself to answer to. If I don't have time for my friends, it is not because someone else is keeping me too busy. It is because I am choosing to work to the exclusion of time for others. If I'm not earning enough it has to do, to some extent, with the amount of time and effort I am putting into it. This is a very touchy point, for women, however. Some of my earning power is certainly dictated by society and the men who run it. ''Last hired, first fired'' is still true for women, and I am very aware of that, as well as of the difference in pay scale.

Choosing to live solo means independence. Independence means learning how to be graciously interdependent. In my new state I have many options. It brings me face to face with my own values and priorities in life. After years of depending on someone else for financial and moral support, I must now make decisions alone. I like the feeling. It is also a big responsibility.

I now find that more and more the evaluation of myself comes from me, rather than from other people. I don't know if this has to do with age, with maturity, or with living alone. Perhaps a combination of all three. I used to worry a great deal about how others saw me. I was determined to please others in order to get their approval. Now I like making strong statements in words and action which come from deep inside me with little concern about gaining acceptance from others.

Women tend to make statements in collaboration: as the wife of or as the partner of . . . . We frequently get punished for making statements by ourselves. As a mature, single woman I can speak out on important issues on my own. The old notion that nice women don't scare the men who dominate by threatening them with ideas is no longer something I'm willing to adhere to.

Having read all of what I have just written I wonder, "Natalie, are you just whistling in the dark? What about the empty house you return to? The wishing for continuity with one person? The chance to discuss the small, everyday aspects of life? The fear of being sick, or old and incapacitated alone?"

A woman who read my first chapter sent me her response in a poem:

> Sorry for me?
> No, this I have chosen
> but lonely, as the summer has passed
> as did the Spring,
> mostly alone.
>
> Oh, to have someone to share
> my evening walks
> movies, tea stops,
> the hum drum
> to fill in the spaces of living
> between dates, business talk, making love,
> working things out.
>
> The casual being, the flow
> of connectedness of patterns
> the easy rhythm that comes in familiar
> secure, togetherness.
> the ache of its absence
>
> The unwelcome tears
> up the stairs of my empty house
> Freedom extends a cold welcome
> on a quiet night.
> My warm body chills on the cold sheets
> of an empty bed.
>
> —Joanne Haynes

It is true that in being alone there are times of deep loneliness and fear. Perhaps I am underplaying this aspect of being solo. But for me, at this stage in my life, those moments are rare.

Overcoming the Fear

It is difficult to tell anyone else how to enjoy aloneness. And if it weren't a problem for me, I probably wouldn't be focusing on it and writing about it. There are times when being alone feels like it will last forever, as though there will never be any more love or support. Loving relationships have ended, a job has ended, a good friend has moved away or died: These are black times, indeed. And each time I am in one of those dark periods, I have the feeling, "I'll never love again"; or "I won't ever trust anyone again"; or "Nothing ever lasts"; or "Just as things seemed to be rolling along smoothly, my whole world collapses, why?" I become bitter, angry, and sad. Mostly sad. I swallow the tears, put up a good front for some people and share my grief with a few special friends. It is hard to be alone at those times. And it is during those bleak months that we are frequently left alone. Reminding myself to have some perspective is important.

There is a life force within us that helps us ride through the panic. Riding *through* the panic usually means letting oneself *into* it quite completely. Go inside to discover the hidden fears. Voice them in words, song, prose, poetry, to a tape recorder, a friend, or therapist. Or if the fears come to you in images, paint or draw them, dance and move with them. Don't keep secrets from yourself. Poke around in the hidden crannies of your fears to see what is lurking there and bring them out into the sunlight. It is not easy. But as with nightmares, fears feel different in the daylight. The unknown is more fearful than the known.

So we get ourselves through the trough of the wave, then how do we ride it when it is high? How do we transform the lonely/aloneness to lively/aloneness? There is no magic, no instant solution. Like everything else, it takes practice encouragement, knowledge, and hard work. Most of all it takes being kind to oneself.

If you are afraid of being alone, try experimenting with *being* alone. Move into it rather than running away from it and see how creative you can make it for yourself, even if that means doing absolutely nothing for twenty-four hours. Try not answering the phone, not watching TV, not having visitors, not reading (if you're a big reader), not writing (if you're a writer), not numbing yourself with alcohol or pills or pot, but just existing for twenty-four hours with yourself.

For those of us who are extremely active and people-oriented, this will be a big step. And the notion is to be good to yourself, not to punish yourself. Be receptive to your surroundings. Try out things you have always wanted to do and have never taken the time to do. It could be carpentry, bicycling, painting, meditating, listening to music, gardening cooking, or whatever.

Experiment with being alone to find what good things can come from it rather than hold it as a boogeyman in your life. Most likely you'll find you like it and yourself more than you imagined. And then you might want to try three days alone, away from the world-as-usual. And most likely you will come back to your responsibilities refreshed and renewed, with greater perspective.

My thought is, if we know how to be peacefully with ourselves, we will know better how to be in the world lovingly with others.

In *Beginnings Without End,* Sam Keen talks about love and loneliness in a way that hits home for me:

"Love does not dissolve loneliness. It only makes me rich in my solitude. It is tempting to surrender responsibility for the self and merge into life-in-tandem—the Hollywood solution. But no corporate merger can relieve me of the necessity of living and dying my own life. I am a single one and merger is for a moment only. If I trade my freedom for succor we cling together and nourish each other's fears of the wilderness, excitement withers and love grows wrinkled as a limb with severed nerves."

Because I enjoy who I am and what I am doing, the clutchy loneliness seldom creeps in. I am excited about my womanness in this world.

Women, I believe, are venturing forth to create a whole new system. Excitingly mature, midlife women, many of them solo, are an emerging new force in this culture. A much needed one! Our high spirited energy will awaken and enliven this era!

4
On Love, Loving, and Lovers

Part One

It occurred to me this morning that any book that is a woman's story is not complete without an honest discussion of sexual beliefs, experiences, learnings, and dreams. The personal openness of other women—both in their writings and in the women's groups I have facilitated—has helped me to understand myself and to grow and change. So it is with an appreciation of other women's openness that I share my own experiences. Putting this chapter in print makes me feel very vulnerable. My hope is that it will be taken as sensitively as I have tried to write it.

This chapter is not simply a story of "affairs." Rather it shows first my journey toward independence and self sufficiency, then my attempts to develop interdependence and finally my new political awareness. If we are going to change our present society where women are subservient owned, and with little power, one place to start is in our love/sex relationships.

As I have thought, written, and talked about my relationships I have begun to understand the larger social significance of the partner relationship. It is important to understand that our sexual expression and our inhibitions take place within a social context.

I have learned a great deal from my three daughters—now grown women—with whom I feel free to discuss some of my discoveries about relationships, sex, and sensuality. We are four very different women, each going our own direction in relation to men and women. Our discussions of feelings and experiences have taught me how to say out loud what had always kept to myself.

My daughters, however, are in their twenties and just beginning the forty or fifty years of being in a relationship. This may include marriage or alternatives to marriage, partnerships with men or women, having children as a single woman or in marriage.

I am writing about age forty to fifty as a newly single woman and the social/political context of midlife women. I need to look at the past decade in order to create what I need for the next twenty or thirty years of my life.

Values I Adopted

I grew up in an era when many of us were given the following messages: "Girls stay virgin until married"; "Early marriage is acceptable and expected;" "Marriage means a monogamous relationship till death"; "Children are an expected part of the partnership"; "Birth control and family planning are the right and duty of responsible couples"; and "Sex is pleasurable if linked with love and marriage."

I adopted those values, seldom questioning them. I remember that as a teenager and young adult I disagreed with the "no premarital sex" but behaved according to the cultural standards.

Now, in my mid-years, I am single, youthful in spirit, interests, and energy. Of course my body is aging. Yet I have as much sexual energy and drive as when I was thirty, which is quite a lot. For many of us this is true. With my children grown I have time to exercise, dance, and care for my body. This has helped me gain a new sense of physical well-being. I no longer take my health for granted as I did in my earlier years. I have learned to recognize my tension areas—usually my gut, neck, and shoulders—and to do something to release that tension when it occurs. I care for myself not to avoid aging or to carry on the myth that youth is beauty, but because I want to age gracefully in mind, body, and spirit.

Having discarded the rules I was brought up with, it is important to me to figure out what I want and need at this stage of life. What are my needs in a relationship? My sexual needs? These two areas are closely related but are not necessarily the same. If I am clear about what I want, I will be more likely to make what I dream, happen.

Goals For a Relationship

I would like to have companionship with a man and to be able to express myself fully—intellectually, sexually, and spiritually.

When I was first divorced, my goal was to feel that I was a worthwhile person without a male partner. Years of living alone have given me time to learn how to be single and enjoy it, to know that I have it within me to make my life full. Now my ideal is to have a relationship that is at once close, committed, and non-possessive. I value the feeling of side-by-side connectedness—looking out at the world together—and a commitment to face problems openly. Within this relationship I would want the freedom to be attracted to other men, and to choose without fear of guilt or punishment what to do with that attraction. This would entail a commitment to openness about outside relationships and a willingness to work through the chaos and jealousy that is so often present. In such a setting there is always the possibility that my partner or I might become more attracted to the third person. Although this is a risky way to live a relationship, at this moment in life I prefer the risk to being stifled by possessiveness.

Women, I find, are at least as much in favor of such open partnerships as men. The myth that women have little sexual drive, have no desire or ability to handle more than one relationship at a time, is slowly dissolving as we discuss openly with one another the feelings we have so long kept private.

Jealousy and possessiveness are not strangers to me. Yet I know that " . . .love is a rose but you'd better not pick it. It only grows when it is on the vine . . . . You lose your love when you say the word, 'mine.'" (Neil Young) I have experienced wanting him to be mine—not wanting the man I am with to be involved emotionally or sexually with someone else. I know the torment and rage I feel when he is with another.

Gradually, however, as I have lived through several important relationships (and some not so important ones) I have changed from being a possessive, monogamous woman needing a partner for my self-esteem, to a fairly non-possessive, independent woman looking for an inter-dependent relationship. I feel the wellspring—the source—of my ability to give and love is deep and everflowing. Sometimes I put the cover on that well or hide the bucket so no one can dip into it, but I know that the bubbling source is there.

Sexual Needs·

In the meantime, without such a primary relationship, I am learning about my own sensual nature and different kinds of relationships to men, sexual and nonsexual. When I use the word sexual in this context I am referring specifically to lovemaking (which may include intercourse but by no means exclusively intercourse). Actually, I believe that all relationships with men, women, and children have a sexual dimension.

My sexual need, at the moment, is to make love often with a man who helps me feel safe enough to tell him verbally or nonverbally what pleases me and what doesn't. I want a man who is not threatened by my physical strength and passion; who enjoys and appreciates my having many orgasms and can feel the same appreciation of my lack of concern when I choose to have none; who is aware of his total sensuality (not just genital), his softness, his gentle, caring side as well as being proud of his thrusting energy; who has respect and caring for me as I have for him. It amazes me that the place where I can feel most equal with a man is in bed, making love. For some reason that I haven't fully explained to myself, I am able to communicate my abilities to give and receive, to be assertive and passive, to soar, to let go, to explore and to share in the mutuality of sexual expression.

Today, as a woman, I feel I take responsibility for my own ability to enjoy my total sensuality and to have orgasms. Orgasm is not my "goal." It is the whole enjoyable aphrodisiac experience that I relish with or without orgasm. I used to believe that it was up to the man to "make me come." Now I believe it takes a man who allows me to feel safe and cared for and who encourages me to enjoy anything I can do with him to help myself get sexually excited. Honestly, in years past, if I did something like rub my clitoris on my husband's leg to get *me* excited, I would feel ashamed. It was alright for *him* to get me excited, but not okay in my mind for me to assertively do things that would turn me on. I have learned that finding ways to get myself pleasured is exciting to the man, also. What a delight to know that what is good for me is usually stimulating to him too!

I now realize that it is up to me to learn how to let go into states of ecstasy and orgasm. A man can help create the right atmosphere, can have his hands, his penis, his body in the right place at the right times, but only I am capable of letting myself go. When I have talked to men about this, an expression of relief comes over their faces. "Oh, I'm not totally responsible for a woman's stimulation and happiness" is the message they feel good about.

I have learned to talk about my areas of shyness and my delight in romantic settings. I like to ask for a shower together, a massage, for oil and caressing. I can put on the music, light the candles. I don't have to wait passively for him to guess what I want. How my lover responds or doesn't respond says a lot to me about him. Are we on the same wave length? Are we both in the mood for the same thing? For long hours of romantic loving? Or just touching? Or a quick fuck? By making my mood of the moment known, I can learn about his moods too.

Coping With Societal Standards

Though I am fortunate to have an attractive body by

Hollywood mass-media standards, there are times when I feel grossly ugly and unattractive. Though men or women may help me feel better by giving me compliments or assurance, in the final analysis I need to accept and love myself, my body. Looking in the mirror isn't the issue: I can be ten pounds overweight and feel I am beautiful. Or I can be the correct weight and feel I am repulsive. My own inner core, that sense of self-esteem is nurtured and supported by others but only realized within me. I've often thought I might be better off if I were physically unattractive. Then I'd know for sure when a man made love with me that it was because he loved me, not my body. As I talk to women who are heavy or skinny or not "pretty" I find that notion to be false, of course. If they don't love themselves they are not sure why a man is loving them, either.

I've also come to the realization that my genitals are beautiful. Women are never taught that the labia and vagina are lovely. Most of us grow up with the notion that we shouldn't look at our genitals. Although women's breasts are displayed on billboards for bras and automobiles, the only place a girl growing up can find a picture of genitalia is in the pornography magazines, and those displays are demeaning to women, not exalting. So, how am I—how are we—to learn to appreciate our own sexual organs? No man can convince me. He can, with understanding, help me along that path, but only I can learn to appreciate me and thereby be free to give of myself.

Having been to various hot baths where nudity is acceptable, I have come to the conclusion that there is something beautiful in every/body. But that doesn't necessarily help me accept my own imperfections. When I use the word "imperfections" I get angry at myself for accepting the cultural standards of beauty. Who is perfect and why should we strive for outward appearance at such cost? I am tired of fighting society's influence—Madison Avenue, Hollywood, parents, and ancestors. And yet, I participate in those values by admiring "beautiful" people.

Overcoming Embarrassment

Reading and talking with my lover or with other women have allowed me to realize much more of my full sexual being. I remember the first time I picked up "The Myth of the Vaginal Orgasm" by Anne Koedt. I was forty-two, just divorced, and feeling happy and curious. I blushed as I slipped it into my pocketbook. "Damn," I thought, "why can't I feel comfortable walking out of here with any book I want proudly displayed in front of me, whether it is social anthropology, *The Joy of Sex,* or *The Lesbian Nation*? Why do I need to hide my interests? What has our culture done to make us embarrassed about wanting certain knowledge? Why have I grown up never talking about my sexual fantasies, thoughts, and feelings?

What Koedt's article said was not surprising to me. I know well how important my clitoris is to me in my enjoyment of sexual intercourse and masturbation. What was surprising was the fact that she had unashamedly put those words into PRINT! My own, isolated experience was being shared with other women and men. Incredible! Five years later I was still having shy, embarrassed feelings as I walked past a women's literature table displaying Betty Dodson's book, *Liberating Masturbation*.[1] Her fifteen delicate pen-and-ink "portraits" of female genitalia were more than I dared look at in public. Now that I have bought and read the book I again say, "It is fantastic to have women drawing and writing about how life is really experienced." Although I have always enjoyed sex and was brought up to feel it is healthy and natural, I had seldom spoken about my experiences or feelings.

Changing Values

Change comes with education: knowledge, self-discovery, and sharing. If I had been in a women's discussion

[1]Dodson, Betty, *Liberating Masturbation*, 1974. Published and distributed by Betty Dodson, Box 1933, New York, NY 10001.

group about sexual experience ten years ago, I would have kept my mouth shut (from shyness or embarrassment), my ears wide open, and I would have wondered, "How do they *dare* say those things?"

Koedt's article was the beginning of many others I have read. It turned me on. I passed it around. I learned how to talk.

My main message to women—married, single, old or young, heterosexual or homosexual—is to read and talk. We have much to learn from each other—ages nine to ninety! Our sexuality feels different to us at different times in our lives, but it is an important part of us always. Whatever experience you have, it is true for you. It is valid. By learning what is true for us and others we find that we have many choices about how to express our sexuality: to stay virgin until married or to have premarital sex; to be monogamous or to have lovers; to become orgasmic through practiced masturbation and pleasuring our own bodies or to stay nonorgasmic; to be celibate or to have many kinds of sexual experiences; to become pregnant and bear children or not to bear children.

It is this opportunity for self-determined choice that makes us free women. *How each of us chooses to fit our sexual needs with our value system is up to us.*

When I entered into marriage, I made an unconscious and, in retrospect, very limiting choice about my own sexuality. I bought the cultural myth that monogamy is part of true love. "Loving my partner so completely," I told myself, "I will not be attracted to or love another man." A strange concept, now that I stop to think about it. Why would a legal ceremony change me from a person who was attracted to and cared for many men, to being attracted to only one? I put blinders on much of my sensual, sexual self. I rarely allowed myself to feel moments of infatuation or seductiveness toward other men. I numbed that part of myself. I inhibited myself in many ways. I lost touch with the dancing, playful, flirtatious side of me, partly out of my own shyness, partly out of fear of being some "evil woman," partly because my husband was possessive and jealous, and it behooved me not to be attractive to anyone else.

How outrageous that we girdle ourselves so tightly! Love has many forms: loving as a child, loving as a friend, loving as a playmate, loving as a lover. What I have learned in the past few years is that if I allow myself the freedom to be open to love, then I can choose what to do about those feelings.

I remember well the day I decided to break the monogamy of my marriage. Although I don't recall my husband and saying out loud "I won't sleep with anyone else," it was an unspoken understanding. During the period of my gray/black depression I yearned for something more in life, in marriage. The "something more" I felt I needed was not just sexual. In our seventeen years of marriage we delighted in exploring each other and in finding new forms of sexuality from our first virgin days, through the ups and downs of child rearing and career seeking. Like most long-term couples, we went through boring periods, times when one of us wanted more sex than the other, and times when we laughed at those couples who stayed late at parties when we preferred to go home early to make love. But toward the end of our seventeenth year when my feelings were "I'm not being heard or understood or allowed to be the newly emerging person I want to be," my sexual energy became a strong moving force. My yearning for something more in life was unconsciously translated into wanting new sexual experiences.

At that time I had been courted delicately, discreetly, with humor, caring, and love by the man to whom I eventually made myself available. I remember driving home one day and saying to myself, "If I pick up one more subtle message that he wants me, I'm going." The next day he called (an infrequent happening). I could tell by the tone of his voice that this was an opportunity for me to come and be with him, not only for lunch, but for bed. (Had it been there before and I had not heard it?) I stopped at a fruitstand on my way to lunch and picked up a box of Bing cherries. "How symbolic," I thought. That tender, loving afternoon when I first saw, felt, and slowly relaxed into another man was delicious. I was amazed at how simple, how human and warm our relationship was. Lightning didn't strike! Wild passions didn't prevail. We were

wo loving friends, united. I was fortunate that my introduc-
ion to sex with another person was with someone who will
lways care for me and I for him.

The thoughts I had after that sunny day were not so
varming: "Have I given up on my marriage? Could I possibly
alk with my husband about this experience, or would the
nere mention of it blow the marriage apart?"

Sexual Fears

I became aware of one of my own fears. Was this a fear
ny husband held also? I discovered that one of the reasons I
ad kept my virginity until I was twenty (not so rare at that
ime) and had not acted on any sexual attractions to other men
luring my marriage was that I feared being compared sexually
o other women. Though I often looked at a man, or a male
ody, and wondered what he would be like in bed; I could
ever bear up under the question "What is *she* like in bed?"
My sense of having to be the all-time lover was paramount. I
vould not only be jealous if my spouse slept with someone
lse, I would also worry, "Was she better than me for you?"
My curiosity was great, my fear was greater, and for a long
ime my moral commitment to stay monogamous was great-
st. My hunch is that my spouse had the same fears. I wonder
low many couples avoid talking and/or experimenting
because of such notions?

Well, after living and loving for five years as a single
erson, I dropped the fear of being compared. Although I still
el that sexual union can be the highest spiritual energy
xchange—even a transcendence of the two people involved—
can also be a fun, playful, noncommital experience that
eeds no comparison. Sexual intimacy can be like other inti-
nacies—fun and important in the moment. I no longer need
o be the best. Each partner, each loving hour is different. I am
ery different with the same person at different times. I find
hat one sexual encounter is not necessarily better than
nother; they are different. That difference depends partly on

what I bring to the experience. If I am in a wild, passionate, highly energized spirit, I may entwine my mate in that response. If I am in a soft, delicate, sensuous mood, I may elicit that response from my lover. What feeling he brings to the intimacy is just as important. Our two energies create something new each time.

I suppose that my greatest insecurity, that of needing to be the best lover, was something of a projection. I was wondering if I would find the best lover. I found a variety of exciting men in varying moods on separate occasions. Perfectionism ruins the fun.

Traditional vs. New Model

When I was first divorced I was painfully aware of beginning all over again with men, as though I were eighteen. How to get acquainted? How to let a male know I was interested in him? How to respond when he was interested in me? What should he think of me...? Would he be a good permanent partner?

This last question haunted me in the beginning. Though there may have been many similarities between my new singleness and adolescence, there was really a great difference. I had lived a rich life: sexually I had been happy for many years. I was an experienced woman, not an eighteen-year-old. But my first reaction to any man was, "Would he make a good housemate, a potential new father to my children?" The only concept I knew in terms of relating to men was that of long-term, live-together coupling. Although I wanted to think about each man as a person in his own right, as a friend and potential lover, as a person who might move in and out of my life, the programming in my head, "marriage and monogamy," was difficult to change.

Some of the experiences I've had have molded me to a new mode of living in relationship to men. I've tried to encapsulate the essence of various relationships:

I can feel wildly passionate and not feel love.

I can feel deeply loving and have little passion.

I can feel passionate, loving, and intimate for the week or month and then be able to say goodbye.

I can walk into a room full of people and within five minutes know who is attracted to me and to whom I am attracted. (Do we all know this all the time but merely deny it?)

When I am my highly-energized self I am doing something to others by merely being present. Others, with the same kind of energy, respond.

I can fuck with a friend for the night and not be concerned if we ever do it again, enjoyable as it may have been.

I can make love with someone I love and be deeply hurt when I know he is with another partner.

I am capable of opening myself to being touched at the depth of my soul by sexual union and mutual transcendence.

The old standards—sex is for love, marriage, and recreation only—don't exist for me (and many others) any more.

The options are so many. We have limited ourselves and robbed ourselves of many different kinds of positive experience by our narrow definition of sexual being. It is particularly important to me, as a woman, to recognize that I *have* those options. There *is* a choice. Women need to be in charge of their own bodies, their own values, and their own sexuality.

Friendship, love, and sexuality are very complicated. Sometimes I choose friendship-love and omit sex. Sometimes I choose friendship-sex and don't feel love. Sometimes I choose just friendship, or just love, or just sex. The important part for me is that I choose. I am in charge of me. It is important for me to allow all of those possibilities into my life and act on

what is right for me at that time. Otherwise I deny much of my essence, my being.

When I find someone to whom I want to give and receive friendship-love-sex, I am ecstatic.

I have been talking about many things: the context in which I grew up, the values I held during adolescence and marriage, and the goals I hope to achieve in a relationship with a partner. I have also shared some of my sexual fears, needs and learnings. I have pointed out how the societal setting has narrowed my vision and influenced my choices. I have talked about some of my internal arguments and conflicts as well as the ways in which I have tentatively resolved them.

In Part Two I wish to give more details of the man/woman experiences which have shaped my thoughts, feelings and dreams.

Part Two

Political Overview

There are two themes in the experiences that follow: my constant search for improved ways of relating to partners, and evidence that there is "politics" in a partner relationship. I believe that how women relate to men is the key which will open the door to their equality.

I have two very strong needs: one, to give of myself, to be sensual and sexual, to love intimately; and two, to feel strong, competent, and effective in this world. In our culture it is difficult for women to meet both of these needs *in a relationship* with a man. Our sex role conditioning and our patriarchal system have made it a contradiction for women to be loving and giving and yet have a strong identity and feeling of competency.

I hope that by sharing my experiences I will be helping myself and other women learn how to move through the transition of living and loving *for* and *through* someone else to living for and loving oneself in the highest sense. In order to *be* in an equal relationship we have to gain our sense of self-worth.

My first chapter on sex role expectations describes how I was conditioned as a girl-child and woman and the result of that conditioning in my marriage. It takes time and practice for me to change my sex role patterning. Now I am learning how to be a more assertive, risk-taking woman in my love relationships. I am trying to learn how to get out from under the control of men, yet still find ways to relate to, give love to, and be effective with them. The intimate relationship, the bonding, partnering, or pairing is the foundation of our society. It is here that the personal becomes political; how we, as women, relate to our partners, plays a large part in how our whole society operates. Whether we are "owned," deferring, serving, promoting our partners—as most traditional American women have done—or whether we define ourselves as equal, assertive, and important in our own right, will make a tremendous impact on our culture.

There is no orderly way to tell about my experiences o the last seven years: they overlap in time and space. Men have been in and out of my life. There have been times when thought I was not interested in the opposite sex. There have been enraptured heights and lonely, sad lows. The following vignettes will lead you through the path of my learnings.

Bittersweet

I allowed myself to be in love with a married man. Why did I hang onto my fantasy for five years that we would eventually become permanent partners? He told me, and I knew it to be true because I knew his wife, that theirs was an "open marriage." He said they had an agreement to maintain their own primary relationship without discussing their lovers. It sounded a little like "go play, have fun, and come back. I don't want to know who it is you're playing with as long as it doesn't rock our marriage boat."

He wanted not to tell his wife that he was spending time with me. I agreed although I felt strange about it since occasionally saw his wife and admired her too. He and I began feeling more and more for each other. I was beginning to want to be partnered with him, myself, but I knew that he was not going to break up his longstanding relationship with her for me. Then his wife reached out to me—she was looking for new friendships. Since she didn't know of my intense love for her husband, I felt guilty and embarrassed when she called. In essence, through much fumbling I told her I couldn't be her friend. She figured it out, of course. I never knew all the details, but my working relationship as well as my love relationship with her husband was severed. He explained that I was such a fantastic person that my involvement with him really threatened her. We opened and closed the door on our relationship several times during the next years. It was never quite the same.

When he reached out to me on occasion, I wondered if we could be lovers again without my feeling degraded. Being cut out of his professional life cut me out of the environment where I was learning to feel competent and equal.

As I felt the relationship ending a year later I said to myself, "I think I just said goodbye to you, perhaps that is why I am crying. As we talked about us, you were honest, and I respect you for that. You said that I would always be in the disadvantaged position in relationship to you. I agree."

I couldn't tell him, without caving in to my tears, that he was a man I could let myself love because he helped me grow. He found joy in my new self-confidence rather than having it threaten him.

We parted. I moved away. He got divorced. I attempted opening the door once again, long-distance. I felt truly rejected. I wrote to him: "You've helped—with one quick slice—to sever my last mooring. I had had a hard time saying goodbye to you as I left the East Coast. What I couldn't do, you just did for me. I feel strangely loose, afloat, and drifting, but shall sail anew when my inner storm is over. I've charted my course by some of the bright stars you helped me see. Thanks. Goodbye." (I hurt all over.)

I felt down, weary, energyless. I was submerged in my own well. I didn't want to smile, or give, or be there for anyone.

How did I get myself into that well? What do I see as I look at that long, bittersweet thread in the tapestry of those years? I see that I would rather risk pain and rejection than miss out on the love I had to give and the support I received.

When I entered that relationship, my idea was to simply have a warm supportive friend become a lover. Yet as my feelings grew deeper I had fantasies of becoming his wife and merging families. (I didn't tell him this.) At that time my strongest *unconscious* urge was to get married again, although out loud I was honestly saying, "I'll never marry again." I hoped for a coupling that would allow me to maintain my selfhood. Fortunately this relationship did not end in marriage. I wasn't ready. I would have submerged myself by serving him, his kids, working with him as my guide, no as equals.

I was looking for new models of male/female relation ship, and this husband-wife team intrigued me. I had neve known a couple who openly admitted to having lovers. In entering into a relationship with him, it felt good that this wa an accepted practice for them. I had contemplated such a arrangement in my own marriage but had not dared to seri ously open the subject.

I was beginning to learn about the complexities of being lover to a married person. I was discovering the tenaciou commitment and bond that exists between married persons even when the relationship is a negative one. The third person invited into the relationship has no rights, no way to make even simple demands. I could have a place in his life—hi marriage agreement said so. Yet when the seas became stormy, I was set loose.

I was also becoming aware that in this relationship, a with my marriage, the myth that "I can't live without him" i nonsense. Although parting and letting go of my fantasie was painful, I was beginning to realize that out of the ending come new beginnings.

During those years I ventured out with others, each time learning something new. Simple things, funny things, exoti things. A friend asked me to meet him at a dark jivey bar Simple? But I had never gone to meet any man late at night. had always been escorted to such places. Could a man come to my home? What would the neighbors think? What did i matter? How would their attitudes affect my children? Wha would the kids think? Do?

Earthy Love

One relationship ran hot and cold, on and off, passionate the forgotten. He was coming out of marriage where anger wa vehemently voiced. He was tired of it. I was leaving a marriag where anger was suppressed. I was through with that. Our meeting ground was nature: woods, ferns, and our own earth qualities.

. . .last night was a new dimension, a whole new sensual reality. I thought we had reached boundaries of ecstasy before, but last night was totally different. I heard myself saying, "This is like the strength and beauty of a deep tall pine forest. The images were all there, bursting in my head: earth brown and earthy love, you are dark forests with dew-dropped ferns; stately pine trees with soft moss clinging, silhouetted against an orange-red sky—elegance and strength reaching toward some unknown space . . . .

A few weeks later, in relationship to this same person, I was saying to myself: "When will I learn! You told me not to awaken you in the mornings for lovemaking, yet I acted on my own desires, not believing that you wouldn't like it. You tell me, 'My body is tired and when you come caressing me at that hour it feels like you are a baby who wants demand feeding!'

"*You* don't seem to understand that I am just *beginning to ask for what I want!* It is difficult for me to risk the asking! I am beginning to realize that if I learn to ask I also have to know how to accept 'no' for an answer."

During the months that followed there were periods of long silence, then deep intimacy, then broken commitments, then nothing. I was mumbling to myself in self-pity and anger: "How totally fucked over can I feel? I ask you to my party and you say you are bringing another woman! At least I said 'no.' Good for me for setting my own limits rather than being nice and then resenting you."

During these first two years of separation and divorce I was trying to find new ways of relating to men. The old monogamous, possessive, reliable, committed type relationship had had many benefits, but I had allowed myself to become stagnant, depressed, and without an identity in that process. As a floundering, gawky, newly single person I was tuned into my heightened sensuality, my sexuality, creativity, and playfulness. I was interested in casual relationships. Yet, when I met (and went to bed with) a man, I expected the same type of reliability and commitment as when I was married.

I was feeling needy and unsure of myself, grasping toward some security, yet not wanting to be bound. I was experimenting with speaking my anger; yet, in this situation, I picked a man who wanted none of it. I was taking the initiative to ask for what I wanted, yet hurt when the response was negative. I was not conscious of the contradictions and paradoxes within me. Like a baby bird just pecking its way out of a shell, I was wet and wobbly and unsure. My wings were not functional.

You are no fool, you must have known!

One relationship was tentative and awkward from the beginning. Then the following scene:

Candles and wine, a fireplace emanating warmth. I was wanting to hear about your feelings regarding us. You were anxious, stumbling, evasive, yet courageous. It was so simple when you finally said it. "I am gay." Somewhere you also said, "Why haven't you helped me say this before? You are no fool, Natalie! You must have known!"

Why? Because in all of my wonderings about you, about us, I didn't let that enter my head as a real possibility because I am attracted to you. It feels nice to be cuddled under your wing or to laugh together. I enjoy our conferences and intellectual sparrings. To my knowledge I've never known anyone who was gay. In fact, six months ago, I wasn't even sure what the accepted word was for male homosexuals. Well, it is good to have it out in the open. Now I know why you were always worried about my expectations. Why have I cried so long and hard? I can't bear the image of you making love to another man. There is something so woman-hating about it. Or is that so? I don't know! I'm confused, angry, hurt. I will have to let go of my fantasies and hopes of being a lover to you.

Out of those confused emotions came some clarity. I no longer have a blind spot in my vision. When someone is sending out messages that he or she is gay, I am open to seeing

t. Changing my perspective was important to me. This man became a friend to whom I was attracted but who was not interested in me sexually. Affection and interest were shared. I began to drop some of my stereotypes and open myself to more people. I began to experience my own homosexual feelings. Being aware that I have them does not frighten me. Being aware, I have a choice.

Previous to this experience I was not open to seeing or appreciating persons who preferred the same sex. After groping my way through this shock and confusion, I was suddenly more receptive. Gay and lesbian persons, with whom I had been friends, began to share their closeted experiences and feelings with me. I was stunned at my own previous lack of sensitivity and perception about their lives. As I listened, I became deeply aware of the incongruity they feel in having to put on a facade for so much of the world—to hide their love from others—and I understood some of their oppression in this society which discriminates legally on jobs, child adoption, and housing, as well as by social ostracism.

I know that I have experienced second-class citizenship by being born female. I am aware that I could not tolerate, at this point in my life, the added discrimination, oppression, and ostracism that is created if one chooses to be partnered with someone of the same sex; but I have admiration for those who dare act on their feelings despite such odds against them.

Don't they think you are in love with your mother?

"You are interested in ME? My God, you are young enough to be my son! Aren't you concerned that all of those people will think you are in love with your mother? Aren't you embarrassed to go to the restaurant with me and hold my hand and smile like that?"

I didn't dare say those things the first time I spent a weekend with such a man. As we splashed and played and teased each other in the large hotel swimming pool, it became apparent what the rest of the weekend would be. For the first time in many years I opened to my playful, laughing, young-girl self. Now I carry that part of me around in my hip pocket, always available to me when the time and mood are right. Two months previously I had undergone an emergency hysterectomy. To me, my scar was a potential flag to any man, advertising that I was no longer a "woman." My twenty-two-year-old companion was more concerned as to whether he would be satisfactory to a sexually experienced woman. We joyfully met each other's needs and overcame our individual fears.

My agism has been tossed in the garbage can as I have experienced several times that caring and fun and love cross the lines of generation. There is much to be said about the mutual needs and interests of middle-year women and younger-year men. The younger men I know are neither sexist nor agist. They have been free in talking about what they want and need sexually, which gives me permission to do the same. They have been energetic, intellectually exciting, and refreshing.

I am aware that if I were looking for a permanent relationship I would find it impossible to live with someone who is in the initial stages of emerging, of knowing who he is, and what he wants. I have been there myself, and have nurtured a husband through part of that process. I don't have the patience to live it yet again. In relating to men in their twenties and thirties, I find it delightful to take part in their sense of self-discovery, yet know that I am not available to them as a primary partner. (I am also aware that even on this topic I could change. There are no absolutes.)

Touch me, hold me

With one younger man—a friend and colleague—we chose *not* to be in a fully sexual relationship. It is a lost art to know how to touch and be tender without being aroused sexually or needing to go on to sexual intercourse. We could hold each other with tenderness, give each other massages in the nude and be affectionate. Although we were sexually attracted to each other there was wisdom in our not having intercourse or letting ourselves be eroticized. It made me realize that the *brain* is the control system of our sexuality or "turn on." If I want to be just sensual and affectionate, I can do that.

How often we deprive ourselves, in this culture, of touch and warmth because we interpret every embrace with sexual overtones. Bernard Gunther puts it well in his book, *Sense Relaxation*.

> Touch and pleasure can be sensuous without being sexual. There is a great amount of communication, caring, close/ openness which can come in mutual sensory interaction; satisfaction. Hugging, and kissing is usually confined to the immediate family or to courtship. We learn to not express ourselves, to be reserved, cool. In a trip to Europe Sidney Jourard counted the number of times friends made physical contact while talking, the average was about 100 times an hour. Returning to the Mid-West he again took up the count. The average went down to 3 touches per hour. Is it any wonder that so many Americans are out of touch? ...Becoming comfortable with touch requires patience and awareness. Experience what your attitudes are, how you touch, what your feelings are. Slowly, if you desire, you can change these reactions and allow yourself to enjoy touching not only others, but the floor, yourself, paper, food, trees, animals, flowers, life.

With this man I was learning how to get and give affection without either of us having sexual intercourse as an ultimate "goal." It is well worth the time and patience to overcome the old model: "If we are sensual together we have to go to bed together." So far, in my experience, it is younger men who have been able to expand their concept of the meaning of sexuality.

Sensuality is a nurturing experience for both the giver and the receiver. I am appreciating my ability to touch and embrace both men and women.

In *Footholds,* Philip Slater writes:

Toward a Task-Free Eroticism:
    It seems reasonable that when sexual gratification is plentiful, orgasm need not be the goal of every erotic encounter from the start but is a *possible* outcome arising naturally as the lovemaking proceeds. In a comfortable sexual setting, in other words, some lovemaking is nonorgasmic. This assumes more leisure time than most people have available and a constancy of physical contact that most Americans would find unpalatable. But it serves as a useful contrast to established thinking on the matter, which is obsessively *goal-oriented.*
    I want to stress that this should not be considered some sort of ideal. The last thing I want to do is to add another "should" to our already overburdened sexual mores. The removal of Victorian restraints from sexual life in America will have been in vain if they are merely replaced by a series of sexual grading systems. [Italics mine.]

Whirlwind

There was nothing slow or cautious about our beginning or ending. We twirled from the dance floor, to instant attraction, to bed, to constant contact, to a delightful two-week vacation together, to a plateau, to another woman in his life, to panic on my part, to a loud, hysterical end. During a period of six months I was wooed from cautious feelings (though I acted boldly) and a certain mistrust, to believing and loving and giving. Although he was just beginning the process of divorce and was not asking me to be a wife, at some level I was still looking for a constant companion and a father to my children. I was horrified at my own thoughts. I feared, with some justification, that I would get myself into a partnership where I would again allow myself to be second-best, non-assertive, and have the man become dependent on me.

Like my former spouse, my new lover was bright, energetic, very verbal, with strong opinions and political views. He
was power-oriented, a compulsive worker, and related well to
students and young people. He constantly flattered me, which
was one behavior I insisted he drop immediately, since my
experience on that score with my husband was so negative.
My conclusion about persons who constantly give praise is
that they need such attention for themselves out of insecurity.
There is an underlying envy and anger in such flowering,
repetitive adulation. I no longer eat it up or trust it. I asked this
man to stop it. He did.

There were qualities in my new love relationship that had
not been present in my marriage. We wanted a non-monogamous, non-possessive coupling and were each developing an
ability to talk openly about our relationships to other persons.
We were able to discuss our sexual needs, likes, and wants and
had fun experimenting and pleasing each other. We were also
able to disagree, argue, fight, and heal ourselves from those
wounds. This was new and exciting to me. However, as I
became more "in love" I became less able to assert myself,
more dependent upon his approval of me, more needing him
"to come home to." In fact, it was the day I was seriously
pondering whether to ask him to move into my house (he was
there most of the time, anyway) that he told me his involvement with another woman left him with very little sexual
interest in me. (He put it more crudely.) I was hurt, angry,
enflamed! I slammed the door on our relationship.

In order to learn and change I need to look at what I
believe in conjunction with how I behave. At that time I was
expounding a belief in a non-monogamous, non-possessive
model for the relationship of two people. Yet in fact it was
painful to me to be anything less than his primary woman.
When he changed so quickly in regard to our sexual togetherness, I was hurt and angry. He was the person who started me
talking about my sexual needs and interests, so I felt particu-
arly vulnerable with him.

At this point in life I was comfortable with *me* having
another partner, but was unable to accept or make time to

work through *his* having another woman who was taking important energy away from us.

It is also apparent to me now, that my ambivalence—that of wanting another husband, protector-type partner versus wanting to be single and learn how to cope with life myself—frightened me. When the scales began to tip toward wanting partnership, I fled. I was afraid that to begin to love him deeply would invite pain, that if I let him into my life he would either put me down, or he would like the people I cherished and capture their attention away from me. I realized with shock that I was still living, or re-living, my marriage!

The fear of losing my identity and self-sufficiency, the fear of repeating my old marriage pattern as well as experiencing the immediate jealousy and hurt, sent me running. In the process I was learning that I can wade through the muck and agony of such an experience, pull myself out into a cleansing rain, and let the sun shine again. I am more able now to find the humanness and the humor of my adventures. The excitement and warmth of loving and the challenge in trying to find new ways to relate was worth the anger and anguish.

I see both humor and pathos as I look back on an advertisement that I wrote at that time to put in the local paper under "Personals." It shows that I was feeling good about myself yet wanting to reach out and relate to men in new ways.

Although the women's movement was certainly in the background giving me the context out of which my new self was emerging, I hadn't read a lot about, by, or for women. Yet this ad (which I did not have the guts to run) gives the sense that I wanted a different type of man and a different type of relationship. Rereading it, I can see that I was afraid I *would* intimidate any man who came in contact with my assertive energy.

> Tall, stately, sensual woman, 42, warm, open, honest, delights in nature, art, photo, sailing, tennis, motorbikes, travel, candlelight, con-

versation, playfulness, and love. Pro-
fesionally making my way in human
relations field. Am happy in my newly single state but look for independent men 25-55, any race, for sharing
all of above. Altho suburban, have
lived in other cultures and dig many
life styles. Prefer single, adventurous
males cognizant of liberation trend. If
you are not intimidated, write and
send photo. Discretion observed.

I distinctly remember avoiding saying I was a psychologist in private practice, worrying that it would scare men
away. I was still soft-pedalling my competence and professional status. It has taken me a long time to realize that if men
are frightened of me for who I am and what I do, I won't be
interested in *them*.

The pathos, of course, is that we are a society of alone and
lonely persons who have so few ways to connect that we need
to place ads in the newspapers for possible partners.

Double Loving

Why is it that when I am enraptured with one man,
another love enters my life? This is not an unusual occurrence
for people, apparently. When in love I am aware of my total
BEING which is open, vulnerable, joyful, and radiant. This
energy encompasses, encircles, and attracts others. So it
seems natural and likely that as I love one person I will be even
more open to loving another.

I had spent two very important weeks with a man I was
growing to love. He was a competent, independent, adventurous person who knew something about sharing his feelings.
He would not let me make him "mine." With him I felt protected without being possessed, adored without being idol-
ized, and respected for my intelligence and style. I was

appreciating his maturity and life experience, his devotion and ever-present passion. Together we were exploring the out-of-this-world consciousness and transcendence through sensuality and sexuality.

. . .I am a kite with a long, infinite string that allows me to go forever high spiraling through star-lit space and yet connect to earth-you. Then you sail away farther and farther, first following my path, then finding your own which carries you on beyond. I let you leave, soar, fly, then guide you to the soft, deep brown earth and life! Life inside me where it is rich shell pinks and elegant purple. . .Last night's loving was an opening of my heart. It is nice to love again; to allow myself the luxury of feeling the openness and warmth in my heart as well as the passion of my body.

In this relationship I felt free to talk about my sexual needs and feelings:

. . .I liked the game we played in bed last night. I was feeling very pressured by your fervent desire. I asked you to pretend you weren't the least bit interested in me and that I would have to seduce you. You played well: you almost convinced me! I became very aroused and excited being the temptress and seducer. Best of all, it meant that our lovemaking was at the pace I needed for that night.

Even in this relationship our old sex role patterns and the demands of society took their toll. During the day as we traveled together the old system came to the fore and I played along: the man takes charge! This old custom felt very easy, in some ways, which frightened me because I knew that adopting it would atrophy my ability to take initiative.

The hotel clerk, the ticket salesman, the waitress, the bell hop, the tourist guide—everyone with whom we came in contact—addressed my partner while I stood off to the side as some sort of limp, dangling, unused appendage. I became enraged: I had lived that life once and did not want to experience it again! The words "control, economic oppression, being owned, being possessed, male-decision-making-power," all flooded my head. And worst of all was the still present fragment of myself that enjoyed it!

I expressed my anger to him: "You give lip service to my feelings about being a second-class citizen yet by your actions you couldn't possibly be aware of the depth of my anger and torment while you take charge!"

We learned from each other's tears, rage, and empathy. We kept the communication open. I learned from him how very difficult it really is to change from that old mode, particularly in a macho foreign country where his ego would suffer if I took my share of leadership.

Complicating matters further was the fact that this man was married. He decided to avoid the hurt and anger by not telling his spouse, although she had made it clear at some level that she knew about me. The two of them were colluding to avoid the issue. It affected me. I felt dishonest and demeaned in the process. When he and I spent a day, or a week together, I knew the three of us were really intertwined, but were not dealing with it. He had chosen to be in control of the situation by deciding what would be best for the three of us. My hunch was that he was protecting himself under the guise of not hurting her. I saw it as a form of domination. I could have taken my power and let her know about me, myself, but to what end? It was his marriage and he claimed the right to deal with it in his own way.

My old fears of being abandoned if the wife found out returned. He promised that our togetherness would not stop if she discovered the truth. I trusted him.

Our agreement with each other was to be open and honest about relationships with other persons, and we honored that. I would much rather deal with anger and hurt than deceit. We both wanted a non-monogamous relationship and wondered how jealous we would feel if another sexual partner came into the picture. Our relationship was exciting and meaningful as we talked about our rough spots, let each other be separate persons, and as we opened each other to new vitality and depth.

So how is it that as I was feeling very high on this love, I let another love into my life? It seemed very natural to me. There is something about living and loving intensely that attracts other people.

Into my life comes a wild, free-spirited, rebellious, tender, sinuous creature. I had simple, pure love to give and an openness to receive. Our time together seemed suspended; our thoughts simultaneous. There was a rippling quality to our love and our bodies, like silver and gold pouring into each other, molten smooth. It seemed like an alchemist's puzzle, almost too much, too alike, yet very different. We journeyed through hillsides, beaches, meadows, forests, absorbing nature, laughing, pushing, pulling in unison. It seemed as though we came from the same roots. It occurred to me that he was my "brother"—the male part of me: the aesthetic, visual craftsman male/me. He was also the angry, self-doubting, world-hating, soul-searching, wandering, man-child me.

...As we lay together and slept, I dreamt. You were dressed in a beautiful black aikido outfit—a loose jacket with satin lapels and satin belt, black pants tightly cuffed at the ankles. I was dressed in white. We were on our beach of last afternoon. There were many abstract people on the sidelines wearing decorative colors—gold, pink, and scarlet chiffon blowing in the wind. A path to the water was cleared as the colorful spectators pulled back to allow a wide path for us to enter. We were getting married. My mother sent a note: "Since Natalie is not sleeping at home with us nights anymore we will not be attending the wedding." End of dream.

I was feeling very loving toward this man, although I certainly did not want to get married. Perhaps it was the black/white part of me I was experiencing—the shadow and the sun. It connected with an intense image I had of two horses, one black, one white. They were rearing up, facing each other with great energy and strength. They were sparring, delightedly—not fighting.

I am struck with the polarity—the opposites, engaging each other. I feel I am allowing the opposites within me to emerge. Somehow he was a part of this process. Are the two sides of myself becoming wedded?

This second lover was also partnered. He chose to be honest with his woman and told her he was going to spend time with me. I felt respected and respectful. His honesty meant that each of us would be taking responsibility for ourselves. I admired their integrity. He had to deal with her wounded feelings and rage, but refused to be controlled by them. His ability to stay open and clear with each of us was a rich, new experience for me. Once he said: "I don't shy from difficult things. I want relationships that nourish individuals. I'd like to subvert any system that has unequal power."

I respected his wife when she walked into my house with flashing angry eyes. She accused me of being needy and without compassion. I admired her ability to confront. I was just as proud of myself for my own centeredness and honesty.

"I was feeling very loved, not needy, when I met your man. I imagine that is one of the reasons he is attracted to me." She said, "You invaded our relationship." I said, "I responded to his overtures. I was open to loving and so was he."

Afterwards I thought, "She is asking me in the name of sisterhood to collude with her against a strong interest of his. Is that right or fair? He loves you and is loving me. Why should I not act on my own feelings? I am open to hearing yours, and relating to you, also."

I also pointed out to her that I was putting myself in a very vulnerable position. That I was risking my tenderness with her partner knowing that their bond was strong. She hadn't thought of it in that light.

On two occasions the three of us spent time together. At first the scene was tense and anxious. Slowly as the three of us began to talk about our fears the discomfort diminished. He said he was glad to have us both together—he loved us both. I understood, because I was loving him and another.

How did I feel, loving both of these men at once? It felt like one of the highest times of my life! However, my fears were many. Did each man mean what he said; that it was alright when I was with the other? My experience had been that the words can be voiced—"I won't be jealous or angry"—but the negative feelings get acted out in subtle, underground, punishing ways. I wanted to believe that it was alright for me to openly love two men. I had been in situations where the man was loving me and someone else, but for me—a woman—to love two men was not as socially acceptable.

As the two men moved in and out of my space there was an initial wave of guilt. "How *could* you?" I asked myself with parental intonations. Then, as communication stayed open among the three of us, I relished the experience. It required time, flexibility, honesty, authenticity, and hard work to live this way. I knew I could be poignantly in love with two men at once.

Why did I become involved with two men who were attached? The traditional analysis of this says: "You do not want to get close to any one person." Not true for me. I felt very close to each person—very deeply in tune, in touch, and even psychically connected. Thinking about our psychic connections gives me goose-bumps.

I did not want to stay distant. Rather, being in two triangles allowed me to express a tremendous capacity for love and at the same time maintain my own private life-space. My unconscious directed my choice of lovers, although I had not deliberately or even knowingly chosen married men.

While living these two triangles, I asked myself many questions and shared some of my lifestyle with a few close friends. I was deeply troubled by some of the comments of my confidants. One was, "Natalie, you are a strong woman. Why do you barge into relationships of married couples? Leave them alone!" I spent many weeks searching my own sense of the situation to answer that question, trying to free myself from the automatic sense of guilt based on the old system of blaming "the other woman." I wrote: "A woman, if she happens to be the third person in a relationship, is not to blame. Who is to blame? No one. The two of us women could point to the man we both love and say, you shouldn't be loving two women at the same time! Yet he does. I ask myself did I do anything to barge in? The answer is 'no.'"

The implication of the original question is that when I feel attracted to a man who is coupled I should rein myself in, or put blinders on my eyes or feelings. Well, I certainly thought of that. I told him of my concerns and empathy for his partner. His reply: "This is what I want for me. It will be difficult for her, and I'll try to handle that. I don't choose to be controlled by the fact that she will get hurt or angry. I want to be with you."

Should I blame him for not stopping himself with me? No, I can't seem to do that, either. It feels more like the three of us were in this together for some reason. Was there something missing in their relationship that invited me into it at this point? Is there something missing in every couple relationship that tempts and invites a third person in—a lover or a mistress?

There is nothing new about this situation: it is as old as

he human race. What is relatively new is the openness and
acceptance of the triangle, and the various multiplications of
hat triangle—two couples, extended families, and intimate
networks. It seems to me that rather than suppressing what is
natural and normal—to care for, love, and be intimate with
more than one person—we are beginning to accept it openly
s a way of life. The social, political and economic implications
re enormous.

To update the "double loving" situation I need to add
hat after a year of such involvement, the man who was open
about his relationship to me with his partner found her pain
and anger more than he could tolerate. He backed away from
me, which of course was excruciating to me.

Rather than dwell on my own feelings of being abandoned I'd like to say that the taste of the dignity and mutual
respect the three of us attempted still lingers. It seems that
each triad depends on the personality of the individuals
involved: the degree of security each feels as well as the values
held. I have since been in a less tumultuous open triad where
we have stayed open and connected.

I don't intend any neat rules or solutions. To be able to
put oneself sensitively into the other person's shoes is a
prerequisite for keeping triangular communication open,
however. It also seems essential to be in tune with one's own
needs and feelings and to be able to verbalize them.

A Non-Monogamous Group

Life is synchronistic. As I was living these dilemmas
some of us singles and couples started a group to discuss
non-monogamous relationships. We defined ourselves this
way: We are moving towards new forms of relationships
where marriage will be open to other couples and/or singles.
Our questions are:

How do persons deal with feelings of possessiveness,

jealousy, guilt, of being open or not open about addec relationships?

What are the rewards and what are the real threats involved ir opening a partnership?

What are the positive and negative aspects for the additiona person entering the couple relationship (in secrecy or openly)?

What are the social-political meanings of this life style?

Some of the initial statements and questions were ver meaningful for me. Various people made these statements:
B: I am afraid to come with my partner if single persons ar involved...it would seem more threatening to our relation ship. I would rather start with just couples who are intereste in opening up their relationships.
T: That's interesting because I am now single, involved witl two people, and finding it very satisfactory. I was much mor available as a married person than I am as a single person whe is happy. So I would have been much more of a "threat" to relationship as a married person than I am as a single person. M: I am finding many rewards from non-possessiveness an non-attachment. I do want very deep personal love relation ships and it is hard to develop these with my partners when am not "attached" to them.
N: Some couples think that because I am single I would ente blithely into their married relationships. They don't seem t realize that for me—a person who respects people—enterin into a coupled relationship is a very risky thing to do. How am to deal with feelings of being vulnerable, of guilt, of potentia hurt, of being abandoned when they have settled their prob lems through me? If I love a person who is coupled, ever though I don't want to be the "attached" one, it is a ver complicated, anxiety-provoking situation.
S: I won't come with my partner because he doesn't know tha I am involved with another man. I want a chance to discus how it is with other persons who keep their additional rela tionships secret from their partners. Is it the kindest thing t do? Does it work out? When is it better to keep these lov relationships to ourselves and not share them with ou partner?
N: If this is part of a growing lifestyle, what are the implica

tions for child-rearing, for community, and for the economic structure of our culture?

We have met for a year. We are still asking questions, and learning how to cope with the feelings of shared relationships. A support group such as ours helps us stay honest with ourselves and each other. Some evenings we talk about our personal interactions, sometimes we play, laugh, touch, and forget the struggles of dealing with the problems. Other times we discuss the broader implications of open relationships.

Some Questions and Insights

The stories of my relationships are largely stories of my attempt to work through two questions. Should I, need I, live alone in order to maintain my selfhood? And, can I be fully myself in a loving relationship with a man?

On the first question, my internal battle goes like this: It would be nice to have someone at home with whom I could share the day's events—the politics of life. It would give me emotional support and a sense of continuity in life.

The other part of me says: being partnered would limit my choices, my freedom, my independence of thought and action. The minute I think about being coupled I start putting unreal expectations on the man—thinking he should supply everything I want in a relationship. I know that there is no such thing as finding all of the attributes I like in one person.

Also, as soon as two people live together they are treated differently. They are invited out together and frequently treated as one person. Couples move in circles with other couples excluding a large portion of the interesting single population. Further, there is something territorial about living in the same space that keeps others away. Women particularly get cut off from having other men relate to them or ask them out.

I have also been finding that having lovers rather than a

permanent partner has some very special qualities. I like the intensity, the high pitch of our hours together. It takes effort to plan our time alone, but I hold that time dear. We set aside our cares, and give each other undivided attention. We plan our precious time carefully. Shall we watch the sunset at the beach? Spend the day on a mountain top with the wind and sun? Or stay cuddled up around the fireplace with wine and food as we blend together? I am also conscious of spending the time talking about any difficulties we are having with each other. So our days and nights, our play, conversation, and lovemaking has specialness to it. There are very few couples who take as much time or have so much intimacy.

There is no right way. But there are choices. Many women have not looked at the positive side of living alone because of the long ingrained negative associations that our society has placed on it.

The second question I am dealing with in all of these relationships is: Can I be assertive, communicate my anger constructively, value myself and my work, be interdependent and use my full intelligence with a man?

So far I seem to pick men who tell me they have had an overdose of anger from their ex-wives so they want no contro-versy. (Perhaps the lack of controversy is why their wives became angry.) It is hard for me to practice dealing openly with conflict when the man steps out of the arena. It takes two committed people to negotiate the solution to a problem.

My strengths—my ability to take care of myself and say what I think—is not welcomed by many men. Frequently I am admired at a distance. I see a feminist backlash as I watch my ex-partners choose either younger women they can nurture and promote, or helpless women they can protect. The male ego (which women have helped create) is still fragile.

For example, I went to a masquerade ball at a Humanistic Psychology conference. This was my opportunity to try out a new "persona." I dressed myself as a china doll in a white gown with ruffles and lace. I tied my hair up with a blue satin bow, rouged my cheeks, and painted bright bow lips. I put on a Southern drawl, batted my eyelashes, played up to the men

asked to be waited on, flirted outrageously, and was surrounded with admiring escorts! It was delightful fun! When I
returned home and thought about the significance of it all, I
felt sad.

It is discouraging that as I grow in ways that I like,
professionally and personally, there are fewer men who will
respond to me. Personal growth for women does not necessarily lead to more options for intimate, committed relationships. (For men, the opposite is true.)

I turn some men away who have not developed their
capacity to be intimate or to relate on an equal basis. If a man is
still calling women "girls" and says, "Women have the real
power because they influence men," I figure we are living in
different worlds. I don't have the patience to continually
educate these men.

I come back to my original questions: How can I be in a
relationship with a man which will allow me my power,
dignity, and self-esteem and at the same time be loving,
nurturing, and intimate? And how can I change the patriarchal system which says that women are expected to
be passive and dependent in exchange for supporting the
male ego?

In the process of looking at these vignettes of my relationships with men I realize that I am part of a revolution. There
is great change in the air and I—with other independent,
strong-minded women—am part of it. At first I saw only my
growth, struggles, pain, and joy as I looked at these portraits
of myself with men. I have been painting these pictures by
putting the bright colors next to the dark, drawing lines that
would bring the whole canvas into meaningful form—my life
form. The paintings have a similar quality. I am not—many
persons are not—satisfied with the old model of relationships. Nor are we satisfied with the institution of marriage
which casts these unequal relationships into cement.

Now that these pictures of relationships have been
painted, I am finding the political gallery in which they need to
hang. Looking at the microcosm of the couple unit opens up
all of the issues between men and women in our society today.

Like most people, I am looking for a relationship in which I can get and give love, companionship, humor, intimacy, sex and sensuality, honesty and openness, and a commitment to work through the troubled times. I also want an equal partnership with shared power. What does that mean? It means there would be a dance of "I'll take care of you, then you'll take care of me." And "first I'll lead while you follow, then the dance will reverse." Such coupling is two autonomous people loving each other in a way that transcends the prescribed sex roles to become something greater than each of them separately.

Sounds simple? It is not. The implications of such a relationship have vast political consequences. The present system of marriage has the covert intent of protecting patriarchy where the white male makes the major decisions at home (the economic decisions) and at the office. We know that when men "go to the office" they are making decisions in the bank board room, in the corporation, as the heads of major institutions, the oil companies, the Senate, Congress, and Supreme Court which reach down into the lives of all persons. These decisions affect whether women can own property, have equal pay, have equal job and educational opportunities, have abortions or deliver their babies at home.

Men seem to loathe to give up some of their power even though the male hero myth of America has boxed them into fierce competitiveness, success orientation, and the burden of being the breadwinner. The price men have paid is that of severing themselves from their sensitive, intuitive, nurturing feelings. The goals of achievement, power, and production as defined in our culture have not allowed men to develop their whole selves. The society we have created has cheated men, while it has oppressed women.

Equal partnership would mean that we, as women, must take our share of the responsibility for the decisions made at each level of society. Equal power and control in a personal relationship will eventually mean equal power in the world.

One place to begin this balance is within oneself and in partnerships. It is in coupling that the personal becomes political. What I allow to exist in my heart and in my bedroom is what will exist in the larger society.

5
Opening

Opening, unfolding, delving deeper, searching inward, plunging to scary depths, discovering still waters—these are the things of which I wish to speak in this chapter.

As a woman trained to give, serve, and get my rewards from the approval of others—particularly men—I found it difficult to begin to *receive* and be truly open.

During the past seven years, while I was discovering my new self—my anger, my strength, my ability to act and do—I was simultaneously experiencing much that is of a whole different order. I am reluctant to label it. Some friends would call it transpersonal experience, spiritual awakening, the merging of masculine and feminine, or becoming aware of the unconscious. I prefer to call it simply, opening.

This private inward journey is at least as important as my activist, outreaching path. I am still looking for the evolutionary nature of this journey, probing the significance of these experiences, pondering their meanings for my place in the universe.

The first experience occurred when I was forty. It was the day of New Year's Eve, and I had strained my back. I wrote about it shortly after the episode.

Skulls on the Desert Sand: A Death Image

The muscle spasm in my back was excruciatingly painful. The pain increased during the day; and by the time the sun had gone down I had tried heat, hot bath, emergency care treatment at the hospital (novocaine shots in the back muscle), and

139

pain killers. By 5:00 am, after a sleepless, agonizing night, I was admitted to the hospital orthopedic ward.

The doctor ordered morphine. The nurse shot me up. I tried to relax, the room began to turn, the ceiling tilted, and I felt drowsy. Good, I thought, it'll knock me out! No such luck. Just as I started to drift into sleep, my body jerked, the pain became acute, and I was awake again. This occurred several times.

At 11:00 am the doctor returned on rounds. "That couldn't have been morphine," I pleaded, "it only made me drowsy, I still haven't slept and it didn't touch the pain!" He smiled, checked it out, said it was morphine, and that he would order another.

The second shot took effect immediately—only not in the delightful ways I had anticipated (comfort and sleep). A surge of feelings and imagery swept over me like a tidal wave. I couldn't hold it back. It was like a dream, but *more real* than real. Objects floated, scenes came and left, colors were saturated, vivid, flowing, bubbly. I told myself—this is a "trip," relax, go with it.

As a psychologist I had worked with many adolescents and young adults who had described their drug trips—good and bad, "ups" and "bummers." I knew the importance of not panicking while tripping. But I had no control over the feelings that swept over me with increasing power. Death scenes flooded my vision. It was Scrooge's ghost of Christmas future, showing me 3-D scenes of what was to come. The MyLai and MySong atrocities were before me in super-tragic color. Maimed bodies, decapitated corpses, children bleeding, mothers dead in tortured rigor mortis. The dirt street was full of death. Ditches were crammed with bodies oozing bright red blood—not the dried-up purple kind. I felt sick with compassion and horror. The scene changed. Swirling intense peacock blue rushed into the picture, a liquid, firey bronze poured into the blue. They merged into intricate patterns, gyroscoping, winding, unwinding, falling out of my vision. The scene changed. The background was now desert sand with low dunes rising in the distance. A white eyeball floated in space—looking, seeing. A brown velvet-textured cow skull lay on the desert sand. The empty sockets of the old skull were also *looking, seeing*! I was frightened. I knew I was out of touch with reality; somewhere in the recess of my mind I knew that this was not so unusual or to be feared—yet I was terrified. "Beautiful!" I told myself, "Enjoy the Dali-like surrealism." But the scenes were of death, pain, injustice, and despair. There was no beauty in what I felt. The scene changed again. Someone was standing beside me, pulling back a heavy curtain that displayed a large movie screen. He and I were to watch (although my memory blocked on what I actually saw) my death!

As the morphine wore off—was it two or three hours?— I was aware of not having moved a muscle. The bedrails were up, the nurses busy with the patient who shared my room. Despair, depression, fear, flooded me.

During the next half hour I knew I was awake . . . . I could not think straight. Reality was back. Yet, like fog creeping into my guts, I knew I was going to die, that others around me knew I would soon die. My dream had been a prediction of my future. The nurses were laughing, afraid to face the tragedy. They whispered to each other as they left the room so that I wouldn't hear the awful news.

My head was swirling. "My god, I'm paranoid!" I was still talking to myself without uttering a word. "How ridiculous of you, Natalie! Everything will be all right—you only have a muscle spasm. Your feelings are way off!" But the feeling remained. I wanted to cry, long hard sobs, but I knew that crying would cause more pain. Besides, I was ashamed to cry over nothing and there was no one to cry *to*. I thought of the advice my good friend gives: don't hurt alone—whether it is emotional or physical hurt. Call someone. *Ask* for help. For years I have tried to bear either mental or physical pain by myself. I know, intellectually, that my friend is right. Sharing helps. Not only does it relieve me, but allows someone I trust the opportunity to give me something. Asking is hard. Should I do so now? Wasn't I being ridiculous to let a drug make me feel I was about to die when I knew that not to be true?

I picked up the phone to call my father. "Dad, it's not my back that is hurting now, it's my head that's screwed up. I need you to hold my hand."

When he arrived at my bedside he let me know I could talk about it or just rest. I mustered up the courage to tell the crucial point: "I keep feeling I am going to die—it was my own death trip." I choked back the tears.

"You are not doing to die; you'll be okay in a few days."

He said it softly knowing the feeling was real to me. He didn'
make light of it. He had conveyed that he really understood
The reassurance in words seemed suddenly unnecessary
I returned to familiar reality.

This episode marked the beginning of my growing reali
zation that there are important messages in our dreams and
nightmares. I didn't know then what significance this mes
sage had for me, but I knew I had experienced a differen
reality. This changed me in ways of which I was not yet fully
aware and which I did not completely understand.

Looking back on my morphine trip, I see that, as the
atrocities appeared before me I experienced existential, uni
versal suffering and the demonic side of human nature. This
pain is part of me, as it is a part of us all, although much of the
time it is buried beneath the activity of my everyday life.

It was characteristic of me, at that point in my life, to
block out the darkest scene—my death. I seem to be unwilling
to experience the diabolic dark side of myself. Even in this
out-of-control state, I found a way to be in control. As
swirled in this other existence, I allowed my memory to fail in
order not to see.

I felt the terror of not being able to control my feelings, o
experiencing emotions as something coming from *outside*
overwhelming me, rather than as a part of myself. At that time
I was a therapist at a college in-patient unit where student:
were in psychotic crises; I could now more fully understand
how they felt as they revealed the excruciating qualities o
their paranoia. I could empathize deeply and yet have a sense
of how to help them back into the familiar world.

So, quite by accident I had experienced an altered state o
consciousness. This raised my curiosity. What is reality? Wha
can I learn from altered states of consciousness?

The morphine episode took place on New Year's Eve of a
year in which there was to be much physical pain in my life
The need to give up and let go came in many forms that year
So often, it seems, traumas occur in bunches. I constantly
observe that physical illness accompanies other stress.

So it was, that after the early New Year fear and death mages I had several trips to the hospital. Each occurred on an "important" day. On the anniversary of my first daughter's birth, I found myself being wheeled into the same hospital operating room eighteen years later for a D&C. Three months after that, on the anniversary of my youngest daughter's birthday I was again on that same table for another D&C.

On the fourth of July I was back again, this time for an emergency hysterectomy. (It turned out to be my declaration of independence. No more need to worry about getting pregnant.)

It is embarrassing to me to admit to the unconscious or "coincidental" dates of each of those occasions. I had given up my marriage and was in the process of mourning the loss physically, if not openly with tears. Most of my tears of anguish and loss had been anticipatory grief previous to my divorce. During the separation year I was too angry to cry.

As I moved from being wife-oriented and child-rearing oriented to being an alone, independent woman, my body mourned the loss of being the needed, depended upon, mother-person.

A *New Death/Life Perspective*

Two years later, after much thought, consideration, and waiting for the right time, I tried windowpane acid. I had listened to the tales of a psychiatrist friend who had found LSD an exhilarating, opening experience. He did not treat such trips lightly. Nor did I. I waited for a time when I felt an inner stability and when I was not responsible for anyone else. My worst fear was that I would go into some insane space and not be able to return. A few days after this trip I sat at the typewriter and wrote. The experience had been profound. I was embarrassed by some of what I had felt, wondering if anyone else would understand. As I wrote I relived it again, sweating profusely, my mind drifting out into space.

It's a hot, parching day on the sun-browned mountain ᵢ Gorda, Big Sur. The cloudless blue sky, gentle wind, th expanse of the Pacific ocean, give me a feeling of solitudᵢ Today it will be okay to try it, I nervously reassure myself. Lo is nearby. She cares for me, knows what tripping is all abouᵢ She said she'd hold me if I ever needed it. That was th reassurance I wanted. Timing is important in life, I know thaᵢ And all of my intake of clues and cues tells me today will be juᵢ right. I am ready. Being close to nature and in a place where am protected from being interrupted feels good. I know I war to get in touch with all of my body, to get completely into m skin and go beyond it.

I carry craypas and paper, water and suntan lotion to little knoll on the treeless mountain. I spread out a mat and s quietly for awhile before taking the tab. Gradually I undresᵢ knowing that I want to be fully present to feel everything . . unencumbered by cloth. I can smell my own nervous sweat iᵢ anticipation of the trip. My own modesty also makes mᵢ anxious, even though I know I am essentially alone in my littl spot, overlooking a little dusty road crawling up the dr mountain. The vast expanse of the ocean is in view. Th occasional truck chugging uphill looks like a kid's tᵢ model. . .that's how far away it is. Yet even that presence ᵢ other beings adds to my modesty. "Don't be ridiculous," admonish myself. "What difference would it make if they dᵢ glimpse you nude on the mountain? It wouldn't hurt them, ᵢ you!" . . ."But I can't help it; that's the way I feel." . . ."Makᵢ yourself get over that stupid inhibition . . .do something aboυ it." I argue with myself as I am sitting pulling off my shirt, mᵢ shorts, my underpants. I stay sitting, curled up knees to ches feet together, chin on knees, just looking around and gettinᵢ used to the whole idea. The tab is next to me. I left my watch iᵢ the house on purpose, but it's about noon. The sun is hot.

The time is right. The little yellow pill looks like manᵢ other pills I've swallowed. I down it in one gulp. I begi waiting. It probably won't work on me; or maybe it'll work toᵢ much on me. Who knows? Stop thinking; just take things in.

Slowly I lotion my body at first for protection, and theᵢ because it feels good. I know my body is beautiful and I don know my body is beautiful. I know everybody's body is beau tiful and I don't think everybody's body is beautiful. Fᵢ christsakes, stop arguing with yourself. I can't help it. I war not to, but I do. I always do. Doesn't everyone? I am not sure. When is the tab going to do something? Maybe never. I stand up and stretch my arms up to the sun and feel the gentle breezes wipe away my sweat.

I get up again, stretch, breathe deeply, open my arms to the world, to the air, to the sun, to me. The colors are vivid: Back in the mountains behind and above me is the egg-yolk yellow field grass. Stately deep-green redwood trees are standing soldier-like in the cooler canyon to my side. With my back to the mountain I view the ocean: first blue-green, then deep cobalt, then fusion with the paler sky. As I sit waiting, I take note of what is next to me. A sturdy gray-green boulder with straight edges is angled upward. Some lichen softens it. Three persimmon-colored desert flowers are miraculously growing from the rock. I admire their brilliance and stamina. Lying back on my mat, I see the wild oats surrounding me, shimmering and quivering against the blue sky. I'm thirsty. I drink from the jar. It dribbles down my chin, drops to my breast, trickles off. My skin feels tingly all over. I lie back. "Just let yourself go and take it all in," I try to persuade myself.

Lois appears over the hillside wearing a hat, carrying a hat and bringing coconut milk and fresh pineapple.

She sits next to me with few words, offering the refreshment. Each sip is exquisite. That's peculiar, I don't like coconut milk. The texture of the pineapple feels good in my mouth. There is just enough sweetness.

"I don't think this tab is going to work on me."

She smiled, "It works gently and not forcefully." She looks at the picture I had drawn while sitting, waiting. It was of my immediate surroundings: the rock, the three red blooms, the wild oats against the blue horizon. She picks up the pad and draws a large warm bird, nesting. "I don't know if this is for me, or for you," she says. Whoever it is for, it looks comforting and protective.

She leaves saying she'll be back later. I ask how long I have been on the hillside. One hour.

I roll over on the mat to stretch. My stomach feels queasy. "Oh my god, I'll probably get sick from the tab. I've read of such nausea. I won't let myself vomit. I will *will* the nausea away. I concentrate on my stomach. "Go away, sick feeling. I won't let you take me over." Perspiration pours out. The hot sun sinks through my innards. I close my eyes; and colors are

swirling in my head. "I guess it'll work on me. Here I go! Don'
panic, go with it." I sit up to gulp more water. I'm parched.
put on the hat Lois left for me. The shade on my face fee
good. Again I lotion all of my body, taking care of every part c
me. Touch is nice. I'm deprived of touch these days. So tak
care of me. I'd prefer if someone else would care for me thi
way, but since there is no other one right now, I oil every inc
of me, myself. How can I know the world unless I know m
own body? How can I be aware of others if I won't allow myse.
to accept all of me? . . . Stop talking to yourself and just dig it.
massage my toes, my fingers, arms, and breasts. Spreadin
my legs I let the wind flow in. I oil my thighs and clitoris and le
go. Stretching long, face up toward the sun, my eyes closed,
let go. Relaxed, energized, soaking it all in. Beautiful. "Nov
that the tremendously sexy feeling is passed, I can concentrat
and let go in other ways. Good." Standing up, stretchin
again, moving with the breeze I declare, "To my body, awa
with any shame, anyplace."

I sit cross-legged facing the ocean and the sky. With bac
erect, breathing long and slow, I focus on the horizor
Gradually a dot, a circle, a center light emerges directly ahea
at the horizon. Lines, pathways of light leave that center
spread in all directions toward me. I am sitting, very aware c
that center, focusing with quiet intensity upon it, and th
pathway of light from me to the center feels strong. I begin
lose sense of my body and fuse, through the pathway to th
bright circle. This is death. Horizon, fusion, merging. Peac
tranquility, unison. Death will be beautiful when I allo
myself to die. It can be like this; a merger. Tears are strean
ing down my face, not in pain, but in joy. I am no longer i
my body.

I'm not sure how long I was there. Five seconds, fiv
minutes, an hour? I want to remember how that felt so that
can go there again. I soothe and stroke my body to be *in*
again. I feel the ground with my toes.

Lying on my stomach I press the earth and warmth int
me. Spreading my arms and legs wide I feel energy pourin
through a passageway in me. It pulsates in spiral fashion u
through my vagina, through my innards, passing through n
throat out the top of my head. It is a pathway opened. Energ
flows through.

Eyes closed, purples swirl. Rich red and crimson purple

Royal purple, plush purple, swirling, moving, pouring. I'm sinking, sinking, sinking. It's too dark, too deep, too far. I'm scared. This is going too far! I can find ways to control even this, if I try. I will not let it frighten me. I will do something to lessen the darkness. I open my eyes. I almost have to force them open as though I'd forgotten how. The purples stop. I force myself to move. I push myself to a kneeling position. The sun is still on my back. I'm drenched. "Make yourself stand up." I do. The breeze dries me. I focus on the hillside, the rock, the three persimmon blossoms. I come back to the *here*. I am pleased. I know how to take care of myself. I am still in control of myself.

I sit again, facing the horizon. Thinking of people I love, I wonder if they are feeling me at this moment. I concentrate on each, one by one, getting the essence of that person, sending out caring.

Lois comes and goes. Eventually I want to be out of the sun. Though I have been nude for hours, I know I have taken care and that I have not allowed myself a dangerous burn, even on my trip. And then I think that even if I get red, it won't hurt much because I *will not let it*. I feel as though I have great control over such things as whether the sun will burn me or not. Mind over matter.

Entering the house (clothed) is my first contact with people. A visitor is talking to Lois. Her voice seems harsh, unreal. I don't trust her; ungenuine. I move around slowly, leaving the house to find some shade. A small shrub casts a shadow to sit by. I am looking over the canyon, the statuesque redwoods. Branches take on shapes. A twisted dead branch appears to be a vulture. I take in the cool. "There shall be sunshine and there shall be shade," I say to myself. Simple. Yet it seems very profound. A swooping line of up then down and up again comes to mind. "There are ups. There are downs. Let them flow." How simple! I laugh. I imprint the line in my head. It's almost the yin/yang. "Oh! That's what it means." Experiencing it is different than reading it. I laugh.

The house is empty. I sit on the bed cross-legged, looking at the rich red, yellow, and blue of stained glass with the evening sun pouring through it. I look to the horizon again. It draws me. "If I want, I can let myself get there again." I'm doubtful. Picking up a book I open randomly to a page and read the first sentence: "Tantra: The Exaltation of Experience:

He who realizes the truth of the body can then come to kno
the truth of the Universe." I laugh. How could I turn to that *o*
thing? That quote has been the essence of my day! Far ou
Beautiful! Weird. The message to me is to leave my body agai
I sit cross-legged, breathing in deeply, out deeply, focusing c
the horizon. Slowly I leave. Eyes closed, I am a sunflowe
"Why?" "No questions, BE." Grey, yellow stalks, tall, reac
ing. Large yellow blooms face the sun, some droop slightl
I am looking at them. I *am* them. Then I leave . . .

    Later
      how much later?
        head tilted back
          sitting cross-legged
            gentle tears of ecstasy
              flowing through the passage
                to THERE. Fusion.

The greatest impact this acid trip had on me was t
entirely alter my view of death. This has affected the way
live. I grew up adamantly agnostic, pragmatic, a skeptic abou
anything religious or spiritual, with a down-to-earth orienta
tion. I scorned notions of god, of life after death. I dismisse
the possibility of psychic phenomena and denied that dream
might be an important part of life. In college the only spiritua
philosophy I ever accepted was Emerson's view of the Over
Soul. If I had been asked to draw a picture of death I woul
have drawn a black box; that is all. Now I have tried drawin
pictures of death in which I am fusing into the horizon, feelin
ecstasy. My sense was, and is, that the strong beam of ligh
from the setting sun on the ocean horizon will pull me into it
orange warmth, and I will sink into a "beyond." I am no
trying to deny that there will be physical pain and a desperat
struggle to stay in this world. But this is not all. I can neve
return to the black-box image. Of course now that I hav
"learned" this new concept, I find many books, articles, an
lectures to validate my new beliefs. Coming to it, on my ow
first, is my way.

    My notes on the morphine experience—the cow skull o
the desert sand, the MyLai atrocities, and witnessing my ow

emise—had been in my files for years, neglected until I
egan to search the meaning of the LSD imagery. By placing
hese episodes in juxtaposition I am confronted with the
ontrast of their messages. The first is terrifying. It says that
eath is excruciatingly ugly, painful, frightening; so ghastly I
locked out the death scene I had been privileged to view. The
ther vision is one of exquisite fusion to an ethereal space.

From these contrasting apparitions I am beginning to
nderstand a very simple notion. If I am afraid of death and
ght it, I will allow the death process to happen; flowing into
, I will experience something profoundly beautiful.

This vision allows me to open myself more completely to
fe. I find the natural flow in life rather than forcing my order
n it.

Why do I allow myself to be so heavily influenced by this
cid experience? I could just write it off as a chemical vision
hat has no real meaning or I could say that this new concept of
eath is merciful self-deception. Yet I persist in thinking that
here will be an exciting, peaceful end to bodily life which is
herely a transition to some organic unity. My answer is that I
ntuitively trust this new image.

Intuition is a way of knowing. Frances Vaughan, in her
ook *Awakening Intuition,* says "When we know something
ntuitively it invariably has the ring of truth, yet often we do
ot know *how* we know . . . .Intuition is known to everyone by
xperience, yet frequently remains repressed or undeveloped.
is a psychological function like thinking and feeling. . . .
xtrasensory perception, clairvoyance and telepathy are part
f the intuitive function. Likewise, artistic inspiration and
nystical religious experience are intuitive perceptions of
eality."

In my process of opening, I allow myself to be aware of
ne intuitive knowledge. The drug excursion, the fantasy jour-
eys, and dreams are becoming significant ways of under-
tanding my life. For example, when I made the decision to
nove from East Coast to West, my intuition and dream life
layed some part in the process. More and more I trust this
ntuitive side.

To be open, to allow our intuitive powers to function, we need to be quiet. Living a life that goes like this—alarm rings news goes on, load of laundry started before going to work, a rapid pace at work, on arrival home TV goes on—will not allow one's intuition to operate. Taking time to sit quietly, to meditate, to recapture a dream and write it down, to watch a sunset—these activities will nurture our intuitive process.

Another concept I learned during my altered state had to do with human energy flow. Mystics and masseurs describe this flow in various ways. I experienced it as an unblocking of energy, like unclogging a pipe. The energy itself seems very different from the kind we feel when we are simply excited. It is a very powerful current which manifests itself as a tingling vibration in every cell. When I am in that state I feel I can "give" it to someone who is open to receiving it. It can be transmitted without touching, by simply holding one's fingers two inches from another person's fingers. A masseur can pick it up from a body that he/she is working on, or it can be transmitted and exchanged in sex.

When I was coming down from the acid high I used this internal intensity to draw pictures with oil pastels. I created images that I had seen and felt. In one hour I produced a collage that was three feet tall that depicted the passageway of energy flowing through me. I worked in an excited state and was amazed that I had made, with folded paper and scissors, an eight-pointed star which I used in the collage. To this day I cannot repeat that papercut. It happened spontaneously, as did the elongated figures (me) with seven openings or centers. Months later I learned that there are seven chakras or energy centers in our body.

When I looked at the intensity of color, the symmetry of line, the unusual forms, the primitive shapes, of these post acid pictures, I could hardly believe they were mine. They were dramatically different from the art journal drawings I had done in previous years. After the acid trip I found myself drawing with *both* hands at once. Because of this, many of my acid pictures, unlike those I had done before, were quite symmetrical. Most of the energy in my body, hands, and pictures started from the bottom and moved upward: lines spiraling upward, arms outstretched toward the sky, sensual genital forms. My image was of current flowing up through my legs, through my vagina, through a hollow tube in my spine, out the top of my head to a point on the horizon, then circling back to me. This is the reverse of giving birth, where all of the energy starts from the top, pushing through the birth canal and out. Spiritual birth seems to be the reverse of this dynamic flow.

At first, during my day on Gorda mountain, I needed to be with the life *in* my body—as I massaged myself and dug my toes into the earth—before moving into the larger land-scape. Knowing and loving my body has changed me. I return to dance movement and yoga to appreciate my earthiness and to receive the messages from my body.

Adrienne Rich's final words in *Of Woman Born* poignantly cry out for women to be in charge of their own bodies: to *think* through their bodies. "...sensuality, sexuality, intelligence, power, motherhood, work, community, intimacy will de-velop new meanings: *thinking itself* will be transformed. This is where we have to begin." (Italics mine.) I have just begun.

Women must learn to understand themselves—to be grounded in the messages of their bodies, and to accept their intuitive mode of perceiving in order to lay the path for a more humane society. The feminine, intuitive, receptive, non-linear, non-logical mode of thinking is a necessary antidote to our materialistic, driving culture. Although men and women alike have the capacity for the feminine thought form, women could lead the way.

The Eye/I Dance of Womanhood

Two years later, my second acid experience continued with this theme. The words that came to me were: This is *my* dance, the dance of womanhood. Again, I was nervous about taking the trip, wondering if I would confront my own shadow side. In my own floating home—my sunny houseboat overlooking sailboats, the harbor, and Sausalito hills— I wrapped myself in a soft yellow blanket which became my cocoon. As the hours went by and I passed through each new metamorphosis, I would unfold the blanket and si quietly allowing the scenes and feelings to flow. I now see the thread which connected each episode: it was the dance o being woman.

As I sit nude with the sun pouring in on me, I am aware of the beauty of women, of female bodies; aware of what it means to be a mother, a daughter, and a mother of daughters. Visions of my mother and my children pass through as though a movie is recapturing important events, both painful and joyful, o our lives together. Words flash: "There is a rite/right of birth passage." With the sun on my face, tears roll gently down, tears of sorrow for women all over the world: woman pain, woman suffering, woman kept *down*. I am feeling the knife-sharp edge in my heart. Sorrow and pride; sorrow and pride! As the teardrops fall to my breasts and trickle down my belly they become both the river of female anguish and the elegant waterfall of woman-pride....Some of the tears are truly golden: with these I bathe myself rejoicing in the delight o giving birth and being mother. I lie down to rest from this see-saw of emotions. I begin to experience uterine contrac-tions: the pushing, the excitement of knowing a human being is finding its way through my passageway into new life!

Suddenly the scene switches. I roll over on my belly, curl into fetal position, surrounded by purple darkness. I am about to relive my own birth. I am terrified. "But there is no midwife here!" I say to myself. Panic sets in. I try to arouse myself, to gain control of the drug to keep me from going into the struggle and bloody scene I foresee. "You're chicken, Natalie. Why don't you let yourself go into this birth experience?" " need another woman by my side, I need a midwife, I am terrified by my feelings of foreboding! I can go through it some other time, when I'm ready. I'm not ready!" I force myself to si up and to turn away from a re-enactment of my birth.

I calm myself. I breathe deeply. I re-enter the present. The center of my feeling is in the warmth of my heart. "This trip is one of the heart chakra," I say. I place my finger tips midpoin between my breasts. I feel the heat pouring forth. Magically, it seems, I open that space in my chest to discover glistening red jewels with many facets. They radiate as the sun catches the ruby color. I am delighted with the riches and am aware that I want to give them away. "There will always be more gems if you keep giving them away." These are "love jewels" to be shared. I feel I have much love to give.

I turn to the big Indian pillow sitting by my fireplace. It is elaborately embroidered with a few round mirrors sewn into the decoration. I look into one small mirror studying the reflection of one eye. I watch as my eye changes shape and color and style. "This is the eye/I dance," I say. Looking at my own pupil I see the eye of an Egyptian princess heavily outlined with burnt cork and mascara. I am in a long dugout boat. There is one man at the end of the boat standing with feet firmly planted, his arms pushing the one long oar which is both paddle and rudder. We are moving down the Nile.

My eye changes. There are warm creases at the corner of the eye. There is a blue depth into which I fade. I am the eye of all women who are in tune, in touch, who look on the world with wrinkles of love and *knowing*. I am aware that women have a very special way of knowing.

I walk to the stark light of the bathroom to view my whole face in the mirror. I watch with amazement as my skin becomes ashen grey, cheekbones hollow. The knuckles of my hands turn boney-white. I laugh. "Hello, old-lady-me!" The image shrivels even more. The wrinkles deepen to furrows. The hair is coarse and straight. I study her (me) closely looking penetratingly into her eyes. "You look like a death-witch! You look ghastly, ghostly, ancient! And yet I like you! I see you are a very, very proud old woman. In your eyes there is dignity though your face is ugly. You are downright haughty! I love your witchy, shriveled, old, prideful face!" I laugh. I open my mouth and look into my throat. I see way down into the deep cavern of her being and view the firey red-orange jewels I had discovered in my heart, earlier. "Oh," I say. "Life begins with the heart-jewels of death."

Later on as I sat by the warmth of the evening fire, a shrouded phantom came floating through the long, rectangular window glass. The image is to my left. I put my hand out as if to signal: "STOP! You are an ugly death! I won't let you in." The image fades away. I feel I have control over how that death will arrive.

Some themes turn up repeatedly. Again I felt the existential universal suffering. This time it was more specifically woman-pain.

Again I needed to maintain control over the death/rebirth process. As in the morphine journey when I blocked viewing my death and in the first LSD experience when I kept myself from falling into the whirlpool of deep dark purple, here I would not allow myself to go into the painful rebirth process. Also, I warded off the shrouded death phantom. Someday, perhaps with a guide, I will give in to the depth of the dark side of me and move through it to some further transformation.

Parts of this trip had qualities of rebirth, regardless of that which I held off. Moving down the Nile in a dugout could be a metaphor for the birth canal. Accepting the shriveled, old lady as my death and the red rubies as love or conception was a poignant experience.

Essentially this day was about Woman: one of the heart chakra, of love, of being aware of the precious jewel-like qualities within woman. It was a connection to the value of women, being in tune with the intuitive way of knowing.

Two Other-Worldly Dreams

A year later, on my birthday, I had a dream with similar imagery.

I open a door into a basement: a concrete room with tanks and pipes in it. The door opens high above the boilers. It appears to be workings of a ship. Water is flooding the room. I said, "The water shouldn't be in this room! We might sink!" The room disappears.

Next: I am looking at a soft diffused sun set over an ocean. The sky is pink and blue. The sun is mammoth as it sets. There is a haze over the whole scene. A woman's face appears in the sky to my left. She has dark hair, a white skin, a stern beckoning look. She has no body. She is *death* beckoning me with her eyes. She floats closer, getting larger and larger. At first I hold my hand up to cover her face so as not to see her. Then I look directly at her. A third eye is set in the middle of her forehead. As I let my gaze settle on her eye I evaporate into the sunset. I say, "Oh, this is what dying is like. It's a pleasant feeling." I wake up frightened however, saying to myself: "I don't want to die, yet."

Interestingly it is on my natal day that I have this dream of death. Again the death image is one of fusion into the horizon.

This fusion, which occurred in my acid trip as well, is best described by Frances Vaughan: "The concept fusion—being without boundaries in one's skin—is extremely difficult to put into words. People who have experienced it merely nod and say, 'oh, yes.' They know what it is. Those who have not experienced it are bewildered by most any description.... When one plunges into the depths of one's own being, and directly experiences oneself as a center of pure consciousness, distinct from the contents defined by sensations, emotions, or thoughts, duality is transcended. There is, in pure awareness, no distinction between subject and object, observer and observed. This, then, is the foundation of intuition as the non-dual mode of knowing."

A later dream integrates the energy concepts of my acid trips and the experience of expanded consciousness.

I am in a flowered houserobe at the top of a graceful spiral staircase. As I descend, I *float* down the staircase with my body still, posture rigid, my feet close together and ten inches off the ground. Down the staircase I float—cool, collected, energized....Amazing!

Next scene: I am in a large marble foyer. A male friend comes up to me after my descent. He says, "You have a golden aura around you." He stands in front of me entranced by my energy and reaches out to connect with it. The flow between us is a super-current! I feel strange. It is like going under anesthesia. I experience a different state of consciousness—a light-headedness. I wonder if I should try to keep in contact with this world or let myself move into the other. It is frightening.

I let go and I "faint." I am rocking myself and rolling in a purple sleeping bag. I am not "in this world," I am in quite another. Actually, I am two places at the same time—still standing in front of my friend who is zapped by my energy and in my cocoon rocking myself, breathing very slow and heavy.

As I awake from my dream I wonder if I really want to re-enter this world. It feels like a long, slow process. I am telling myself, "Your pulse is *very* slow. You were near death. Or was it anxiety? Or something else?" I am impressed and confused by the experience.

This dream is the second experience I have had being "out of my body," or feeling that I was actually two places at one time. Of course this was "just a dream," yet on waking I realized I had experienced something totally new.

Reading Robert Monroe's book, *Journeys Out of The Body*, gave me the sense that such states may exist for some people. I read with amazement how he could leave his physical body, travel elsewhere, and look back at himself lying asleep. My dream had much of that quality.

This dream also illustrates the concept of transmitting energy from one person to another by simply focusing it and being open to receive it.

I perceive the meaning of these journeys on four levels: as ego-death, as a life transition, as an awareness of death as fusion, and an awakening to the possibility of other realities.

It has been pointed out to me that loving someone deeply contains elements of ego-death. When I am connecting with a partner in a loving/giving/transcending way, I am also letting go of a part of myself. The birthday evening when I dreamed I disappeared into death's third eye was a time of profound personal fusion with my lover. It was a giving up of myself to another. We were also saying farewell for two months.

At this time I was in a life transition period from an active, practical life to an inward, opening journey, a search for a more spiritual life. There is an ego-death in this process, also. The death image could be the part of me that needs to let go in order to move into a new state of being.

The most encompassing notion is that my experiences and images are a new awareness of our connection to other levels of reality.

The Alone Pilgrimage

Several other dreams and guided fantasy trips over the past few years have changed my view of myself and the world.

> Dreamt a lot tonight. Woke up breathing heavily, again. Had dreamt of the passageway of air *through* me—from my vagina through my spine to an opening in the top of my head. I was highly energized. Much like my acid experience. Thought about getting up to read or write, but didn't. Went back to sleep and dreamt of my oldest daughter. The dream seems to be about me, disguised as her. I embarked on a long, three-stage journey, just as Siddhartha did. Wrapped in a white sari, walking along a winding path up steep mountains, alone, calm, and with some sadness, I am in Search Of My Soul.

Months later a friend trained in psychosynthesis led a small group of us on a guided fantasy, helping us get into a quiet, meditative state and giving some very brief instructions.

> "Find yourself on a lake." I picture a small clear lake on top of a mountain with pine trees surrounding it. There are a few boats and people. I am swimming nude. "Calm any waves down with the calming of your thought." The ripples in the lake settle. I feel serene. "Find your way across." I find myself swimming, coming ashore where there are trees with moss, ferns, and the pungent aroma of pine needles. I walk slowly on the cushiony ground. I come to a small footbridge across a small stream. I had seen this bridge in my Siddhartha dream. As I cross it I see a white, snowcapped mountain to my right. There is a flat area to the left of the lake. I can't look to the left. All my weight and concentration are on the right side. The

mountain path is going up to the right. I walk through fog an
come to the bright, sunny, cold mountain. "Find your wise ol
person at the top." I experience an unbelievable radiance!

One long-stemmed red rosebud, large, but not oper
appears. I see it and am astounded: This is no mere image. It i
incredibly real. It disappears. I try to bring it back, but it ha
gone. I find myself saying, "That's strange. I know what it i
like to be a sunflower from my acid trip, but being a rosebud i
new." Back on my path, I never get to the top of the mountain
I find a large, oval snow cave, smooth and womb-like, abou
three-quarters of the way up the mountain. I sit there, almos
facing the sun, but not quite. Nothing is symmetrical. Every
thing is leaning toward the right. I want to straighten th
"picture" up and see the symmetry. It would mean twistin
my body to the left and looking into the sun.

To me, the most astounding part of this fantasy wa
"seeing" the rosebud. I had never experienced that kind o
vision before. How does one describe the presence of a realit
that is not visible to the others around?

One could psychologize and call it a hallucination. Suc
labeling has never been part of my personal or professiona
way of describing life. In this case it would demean the experi
ence as "false" perception. If I write it off as false I am closin
myself to the possibility that objects can actually becom
"present" to us in ways other than our usual day-to-da
experience. I wish to stay open to the notion that the rosebu
was momentarily there. If I trust my *experience* of it, i
was there.

The search, the uphill climb, the aloneness, the crossin
of a stream—these are evident in both the dream and th
fantasy. Finding my niche three-quarters of the way up th
mountain symbolizes my place along my life line. Thes
images seem to describe my life stage, now, as did th
previous dream of where I was in search of my soul.

It interests me that all of my energy, in the fantasy, wa
directed toward the right side, and that I couldn't turn to se
the left. This image occurred during the first eight months o
my rerooting in California, also. Almost all of my efforts wer

to establish myself professionally. Starting from scratch to build a reputation of competence as a self-employed person took much of my time. I was being practical, assertive, logical, and all of the things I associate with the right side of my body. I was ignoring, to a great extent, my intuitive, left side.

Inner Polarities

It was during this same eight-month period that I was spending time at Anna Halprin's Dancers' Workshop getting re-acquainted with my body and my delight in moving. I had loved dancing as a child but had put it aside as I became a "responsible adult." I look at my notes from the workshop training program and see similar themes appearing: the concept of circular energy, the confrontation of death, the dialogue between the right and left, male/female, logical/intuitive aspects of myself.

I need to explain the process of drawing self-portraits in order to make my dance of these self-portraits comprehensible. I had drawn two life-size images on long sheets of paper. The first one depicted body sensations I had experienced in class for several weeks. The second was a right/left portrait stimulated by exercises focusing our attention on feelings in each half of our bodies. I had drawn it by folding a six foot piece of paper in half lengthwise. With my right hand I chose colors to depict the emotions and sensations of my right side. Turning the folded paper over, I then picked colors with my left hand to draw the outline of my left side. When the paper was unfolded the two halves of myself were facing me in full contrast. My journal notes follow:

It was an emotional day for me at Dancers' Workshop. I "activated" my self-portraits. That is, I danced or enacted the themes I had drawn of myself. This ten-minute performance was video-taped, which allowed me to watch my own performance later. It was a deeply moving, shaking, trembling thing

Place a blank piece of paper first over the left side then over the right side of the self-portrait.

Left Side	*Right Side*
I am free, flowing,	I am rigid, stern, judgmental
joyous, lyrical,	I put myself down,
sensual, and spiritual,	blame myself,
gliding through space.	and have tension spots.

for me to confront myself and to move-act-do-it in front of everyone.

I tacked my two portraits on the wall. They are bigger than life-size nude images filled in with color, lines, and symbols that portray my feelings about myself. One picture depicts a lot of height, warmth, sensuality, and also shows severe pain in my gut and a black sun (death) descending in the background. The other portrait is a right/left image of myself. As I watched the video-tape feedback of myself, I saw me: look at myself—my full size—in amazement, wonder, appreciation, and fear; grasp my stomach in agony; fold over in pain, and feel the full sword-like impact in my gut; gradually reach up and out letting out a wrenching sound.

Dancing it and watching myself on video was a shaking experience. It also felt like a release.

On the video tape I saw myself focus on the black setting sun in the picture which was over my right shoulder. I started to dance my own death scene. I was not very convincing to myself. I didn't allow myself to get into the feelings very deeply. It was a surface performance—only a beginning. I found it too frightening to carry very far.

This self-portrait also showed "hot-dots" on the palms of my hands. I moved to dance the meaning of these spots. I slowly took energy from the palm of one hand and transferred it to the other. This was done carefully, gracefully, with much intensity. Back and forth—my whole body moved as I gently lifted the energy from one palm and stretched it, thread-like, into an arc, letting it seep into the palm of the other hand. I repeated this many times with increasing speed. It was as though I were moving a small ball of fire from one hand to the other while dancing freely around the floor.

I said goodbye to that picture and moved to the right/ left portrait of myself. Dancing the right half of me was excruciating:

I am rigid, I am stern. I point at myself, blaming myself, putting myself down. I shake my fist at myself. I stomp my foot at myself. Inside I am trembling. I feel panic. I put myself on the floor and drag myself, pounding my fist. The right side of me is judgmental, stern, and hard on myself. I exhaust myself. Then I rise and move to enact the left side of me.

I am free, flowing, joyous, lyrical, graceful. I gradually relax. I feel my spiritual, sensual self gliding through space. I

enjoy myself for many minutes. I make eye contact with some
of the people in the room. It is the first time I have dared look at
anyone. As I close this dance of myself I move to become part
of the audience sitting on the floor. I feel very exposed, as
though everyone had viewed an inner me that I was just
beginning to see myself. I feel I know myself better.

By exaggerating the two sides of myself—my polarities—
I feel more integrated.

To some people it may seem strange that I talk about the
polarities within me, or the right/left sides of me. To others it
will connect with their own experience. It is the continuous
dialogue between these two aspects of myself that is much of
my source for creativity. If one side of me totally dominated
the other aspects of me—that is when I would begin to worry
about myself. If I should become completely logical, linear in
thinking, pragmatic, moralistic, and stern, I would find
myself single-minded and dull. If I were predominantly intuitive, receptive, sensual, and spiritual, I would feel un-
grounded, spacey, and strange. It is the occasional face-to-
face confrontation of both parts of myself that stirs deep
excitement. Instead of asking myself, "Which shall I be?" I am
learning to ask myself, "What will I be if I push my boundaries
in both directions?"

One of the most important dreams of my life seems to
symbolize this. The image I had was so startling that I sat
straight up in bed before I realized I was awake. The next
morning I drew a picture of the dream image. It is difficult to
describe the intensity with which I felt it.

Two black cobras with tails coiled to support their upright
bodies face each other, staring directly into each other's eyes.
Their triangular heads jut forward from highly arched necks
frozen in this encounter. Instead of the cobra hood these
snakes have large oval breast plates dramatically striped with
yellow and black. A magnetic push/pull pulsation vibrates
between the serpents as they are poised in this striking stance.
They are framed, in the background, by an immense, golden
full moon.

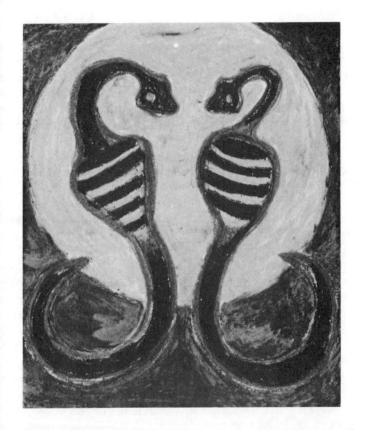

That apparition has never left me. Drawing the image has
elped me remember it. The intense, positive energy between
he two snakes had a powerful impact on me. These two
reatures are of almost equal strength and size. The snake on
he left is proud and strong, with neck and head reaching
orward. She has five yellow stripes, is slightly smaller, and
er head is less assertive. Her neck is not as firmly attached to
er body as her twin's. In drawing this picture I was totally
nconscious of their differences until months later. Now I
vonder if the dream is partly a statement about the new-
ound strength of my psychic, feminine side. The full moon in
he background is an integrating circle encompassing the
odies of both.

After dreaming this I became more aware of the snake
ymbols in museums and books. They abound, of course. In
ung's *Man and His Symbols*, he talks of the serpent as existing

in the myths of every culture as the symbol of the source of energy, of cosmic forces. The snake assumes many forms including the two serpents intertwined around a wand which becomes the caduceus (used as our medical symbol), the symbol of healing, of fluidity, and of opposing forces balancing one another.

The snake, I understand, is also a symbol of transcendence—a mediation between earth and heaven. In my middle age I am more aware of that which is not earthbound.

My dream contained the opposing forces within me framed by the larger feminine symbol, the full moon. When these forces confront each other they create a dynamic vital energy.

A year later, I was a guest at a Jungian group meeting with Katherine Whiteside Taylor. (I am discovering in writing about these events that the full moon of January and February are particularly important times in my life.) After some quiet meditation in her living room, she guided us on a fantasy trip. Her words were something like this: (She gave us plenty of time between sentences to let our imaginations roam.) "You are going up a path...you are walking through a woodland...you get to an opening and there is an image of a god before you...it is benevolent. You feel the urge to kneel down before it and tell the god of your deepest yearning...you spend time there and then get up and return on the path. What do you see?"

I found my way through the thicket into the open field and saw a stone-grey totem that was stern, stiff, and unyielding. When I looked again it had dissolved and changed into a stone-grey goddess with a large belly and rounded hips. Her shoulders were softly sloping. Her hair was long and flowing to the ground. S/he was sitting like a Buddha. It merged to be both male and female. Penetrating blue eyes looked deep inside me. Then the eyes turned compassionate brown. I didn't kneel before the god/dess. I merely stood with open hands and spoke of my deepest yearning: "LOVE."

I turned to go down the narrow sandy path. A red-bellied garter snake slithered across my path, joyfully. I laughed at the friendly sight. It burrowed under the grass at the base of a wild white iris. I moved on.

The path led down through undulating, soft green hills. They seemed familiar. I looked toward the right and saw, on a high knoll below, lovers joined. They lay still, quiet, un-moving. A hawk soared and swooped above, coming close but not landing.

After taking in the quiet entwined unity of the lovers, I looked down into the valley below and saw a black horse and a white horse. They reared up facing each other—confronting, pushing excitedly, almost dancing with each other on their hind legs. The energy between the two was strong, vital, electric. I moved on.

The path curved downward. I came to a small, clear pond. I knelt before it to find my reflection. At first I saw the long blonde hair to the ground, as in the god/dess. That image left quickly. Then all I could see was an Egyptian eye, with charcoal eyeliner, deep and mysterious. I entered the pupil . . . something small dropped into the pond causing a rippling of lines. Instead of the ripples moving in concentric circles they moved from a base point up and outward, reaching. As the lines flowed up the image turned into a three dimensional form to become an ivory-white magnolia blossom.

After hearing of my journey, Ms. Taylor remarked that the imagery seemed full of opposites. If I turn away from the feelings of the fantasy and look at the imagery, I see that the male buddha turns female, the snake and the white iris are opposites, the male and female lovers are intertwined, and the black and white horses are confronting each other. At the end of the fantasy concentric circles become radiating lines from a base point. A unifying magnola blossom emerges.

The feelings I had during those ten minutes were of outreaching compassion and inner depth and love. I felt whole.

An Altered Perspective

These experiences have altered the lens from which I

view the world. The drugs—the morphine and LSD—which began these journeys seemed to have released me from some old values, familiar thought patterns and my pragmatic, linear way of thinking. They allowed me to open myself to my unconscious and perhaps an awareness of an outer, cosmic consciousness. Or possibly the drugs just speeded up a process to which I was already unconsciously committed— that of peeling the layers to *get* to the unconscious.

Being newly aware of a different kind of energy, I can find ways to get to that space without drugs—through meditation, dance and movement, sexuality and art.

This opening process has allowed me to find new path ways of energy within myself. I experienced that we can transmit human energy to others and can possibly be two places at the same time.

My notions about reality have altered. Ram Dass says "Part of the process of awakening that we're going through is the recognition that the realities which we thought were absolute are only relative....We are living simultaneously on a number of levels...to define yourself as being within any one plane of this baklava is to impose a limiting condition, and you are then less than free...part of the key...is the process of allowing other kinds of knowing to be real for you, other than the ways you know through your five senses and you thinking mind. Sometimes we call it the intuitive mind."

For me, the opening process is tuning in to my intuition and accepting its importance.

Through dream images and altered states of consciousness I have seen that death can be an ugly, painful process of holding on or can be an exquisite fusion into a unity with the universe.

I am powerfully aware of the importance of Woman, or the feminine principle, and that the absence of this mode of experiencing and viewing the world is much of what is causing our society to crumble.

As I near fifty my transition in life seems to be the journey in search of my soul—or inner truth. This involves, as my last fantasy so clearly explains, an integration of the polarities of the opposing forces within.

6
The Impact of Women on My Life

Part One
Daughters and Mothers

It seems appropriate that I should begin to write about women—what women have been to me in my life—as I sit on a seventh-floor balcony overlooking a womb-shaped bay watching the ebb and flow of the Pacific.

The ocean, to me, is woman/mother—the place where we all began. She is deep, mysterious, powerful, gentle and soothing, responding to the pull of the moon.

I watch the long surging wave crest, foam, fold under; come pounding down then gently ease to shore; sink into the sand; and pull back to start the cycle again. I think of women struggling for centuries to be accepted and treated as equal persons: waves of feeling surging to full height; anger breaking, foaming, pounding with great impact—anger making itself heard. Then, retreating as we ease toward a longed-for shore and become absorbed again in the sand of the male-dominated world. Then, pulling back into the ocean of woman-experience, we gain calm and momentum to surge and pound the rocks once more. Centuries of pounding will gradually reduce the rocks of opposition to sand. It is a long, tedious procedure.

And as I sit at the base of this uterine-shaped bay looking through the passageway to the horizon, I think of birth and birthing. Even the profile of the hill I see appears to be a woman lying on her back, knees raised as though she is about to deliver.

I am on vacation with three other women—two of my daughters and one daughter's lover—each of us with her own interests: musicians, teacher of women's studies, psycholo-

167

gist, artists and craftpersons, photographers, writers, scientist, women lovers and women without their male lovers.

Among the four of us there is talent, strength, and beauty. We share a great deal and yet we are very separate. The days pass smoothly, with few hassles and a minimum of tension. As women who have laughed and cried together we move in and out of each other's physical and psychological space with ease. I have come to realize over the years that the togetherness of women who have self-esteem is a very potent force.

Frequently people ask me with a twinge of pity, "What, you have no sons?" I have never felt any self-pity about having three daughters. Quite the contrary. I have learned a great deal about myself through loving them and watching them develop. As I come to understand their ideas, their life styles, their inner depth, I gain further respect for women and for myself.

I am writing this chapter to look at my relationships with women. I have explored my relationship with men and the male-dominated world. But it is only as I understand my relationship to women that I can fully see myself. As I have opened myself to listen to women's struggles, I have learned to care more about myself. I am not sure which came first— being able to *hear* women or to hear my own self-worth. I am aware, however, that the support of women has changed my life.

I start with some basic questions:

How did my relationship with my mother influence me? What was my birth like and how did I relate to her as a girl?

Why and how did my initial childhood-teenage camaraderie with girls change to disinterest and eventually contempt for most women?

When and how did I begin to swing back into balance—having women confidantes and colleagues?

What and who has influenced me toward a new caring for and understanding of women?

Mother and Me: A Look Into the Mirror

My own birth process was not difficult, so I am told. But immediately after my birth my mother started hemorrhaging. Since there were no blood transfusions in 1928, her life was in severe danger. I wonder, now, how much impact it had on each of us that my life nearly cost her hers. "You nearly died in order for me to live, Mom." A weighty thought . . . symbolic, perhaps, of the push-pull we have had with each other.

When I was in college I used to get birthday letters from my father telling me how much he loved me and what a happy but frightening day it was for him when I was born. He had come close to losing his sweetheart. After several such greetings I asked to be spared the gory details of my after-birth.

There have been two or three times when I have come close to remembering my birth process. But I have turned away from these memories—still afraid to relive it.

Since the first child in our family was a son, a girl was welcome. My mother has often said that my brother was such a hyperactive child she was relieved to have a daughter who was easier to care for. I believe she was also delighted to have a little girl to keep her company in the kitchen and the laundry room, and when going to the store. I have fond memories of helping her make cookies, trying my hand at the mangle-iron (a roller iron on which she ironed sheets—imagine ironing sheets!). In the back yard I would help her hang up the clothes so they would smell fresh.

With my neighborhood chums I went to our attic to search the musty trunk for dress-up clothes. I found her high-heeled shoes, some long strings of beads, and an old lace curtain I used for a veil with a long train flowing behind. Putting these on I added a touch of her lipstick and enjoyed being a "grown-up lady"—a sign of adoration and a desire to be like my mother.

Mother made clothes for my dolls. One Christmas she went to great lengths to secretly make me an elaborate Southern-belle hoop-skirt with ruffles, pantaloons and a bonnet. This was my most cherished wish come true! As a girl-child I was warmly cared for and appreciated by my mother.

In August 1977 I wrote a poem to my mother. It came flowing out of me as I was standing on an expansive beach—a re-awakened awareness of my childhood love for her.

I read this poem aloud to her at a women's meeting titled "Women, Sung and Unsung" at the annual Humanistic Psychology Conference. I had sent her the poem so that she would have an opportunity to prepare a reply for our daughter-mother presentation. There were many of us who chose to honor special women in our lives at this program. Here is what I read:

> People frequently ask me, "Are you Carl Rogers' daughter?" It has taken women's groups like these to raise my consciousness to give the appropriate answer to that question, which is "Yes, I'm the daughter of Helen and Carl Rogers."

To Helen Elliott Rogers   August 28, 1977

To Mother

I have spoken with many women lately
    About being a daughter.
I have heard these words:
    "My mother was too depressed to love me."
    "My mother was too busy to be with me."
    "My mother didn't know how to love."
    "My mother didn't want me."
    "My mother overprotected me."
I could go on and on with what I've heard.
I am here to tell you what I appreciate about you,
    My mother.
When I was a little girl, you were warm and soft.
You smelled good when we cuddled.
When I fell and scraped my knee, you would kiss it
    And "make it all better."
You were there for me.
Good smells came from the kitchen.
You took joy in feeding us with good food.
You gave your love and warmth freely, protecting me
    From real harm without fencing me in.

I knew I was wanted and cherished.
When I was gawky and shy you encouraged me to stand tall
     And be proud.
You saw me as beautiful which helped me to see
     My own beauty.
You allowed me to leave you with a spirit that let me know
     I could always return.
Your way of being let me know that motherhood is a
     Joyous part of a woman's life.
I took all of that in, as part of me, for which I am grateful.

The love, concern, and nurturing you have given to me and
     Many others continues to be passed on.
You have a sense of home—a serene, aesthetic environment.
You have created beauty with your artistic endeavors.
You have been available to give of yourself and
     Be supportive to your husband and children.
You have been an outspoken leader for the right of women
     To choose whether and when they will get pregnant.
You have given your time and money generously
     Without strings to foreigners, friends, relatives,
     Your children and grandchildren.
You have worked long and hard to create the atmosphere
     In which your children and husband could flourish
     To full bloom.
You are a unique and beautiful woman with pride,
     Strength, and dignity.
You are a symbol of the many unsung women in the world.
I want to give you the credit you deserve,
     Here,
     With love.

                                             Natalie

To me, *feeling* this poem inside of me was a long time in
coming. In the years between my easygoing childhood and
the present, I felt a lot of anger toward my mother. Then most
of the anger disappeared and I took on what I perceived to be
her emotional pain. So the poem was my way of coming full
circle: from childhood adoration to adult anger to mature
appreciation.

Her response, which she read to the eighty women sitting in a semicircle on the floor, is more down to earth, and acknowledges the fact that we have had different opinions and differing values. Her reply:

Dearest daughter Natalie,

I have read your beautiful tribute to me with great appreciation and love. You have expressed, very eloquently and with much caring, what I have meant to you through the years. Only a few mothers would have daughters who would or could express to them so sensitively what you have been able to see and tell me about myself as a person. I accept it all with a great feeling of warmth and with all the love that goes with it. And I believe all that you say is true.

I feel I want to complete the picture of me as a person by adding a few thoughts of my own which will show that I am also very human.

There have been times when I have not listened to you in an empathic way.

There have been times when I have been too authoritative and have attempted to force some of my values on you.

There have been times when I have disagreed with some of the paths I saw you taking when you were maturing or breaking away from the parental pattern or influence.

There were times when I have felt as misunderstood by you as you have felt about me.

There were times that I have been too judgmental and have said things I wish I hadn't said. I have always been a very forthright, outspoken person, which sometimes gets me in trouble. I must be true to myself. But there have been times when I have wished I had given more consideration to my thoughts before I spoke them.

There were times when I have become very discouraged with myself as a person—feeling unable to "play the cards that had been dealt me," especially with my physical illnesses.

I am saying all this to remind you that I am not always courageous and have many human frailties along with all the beautiful attributes you have given me.

As to your phrase of being one of the many "unsung" women, I wonder if I can fully go along with that. If to be "unsung" means not getting scrolls, and plaques, and awards of merit, it is true I have none of those.

But I feel that all my life I have done what I wanted to do. I had choice and, for me, my choices have been very rewarding in themselves:

In raising two beautiful, talented children of whom I am inordinately proud;

In helping my good husband to reach his goals and have impact and influence in his field of endeavor;

And in feeling that perhaps a little of me as a person has brushed off on those with whom I have come in contact, is for me a great reward in itself and a large part of my immortality.

When I think of the many fine travels and the happy

decisions and experiences Carl and I have had throughout these 53 years, the care and love that my husband and my children and my grandchildren and friends have given me, really do not feel "unsung." The rewards have been great and I wish for all women as fulfilling a life as I have had.

Throughout all these years my love for you and yours for me has continued to grow and I'm sure it always will.

With much appreciation,

Mom

The best part for me was when she read the line, "and accept all of what you say as true." The audience burst into spontaneous applause, which seemed to be an acknowledgement that most women seldom take in or speak out about their personal strengths.

I suppose the thing I have disliked the most about my mother is her self-deprecation, particularly in her middle and older years. And who knows when it began? It was part of the expected role in her life as well as mine.

As I moved from childhood to adolescence, my uncomplicated admiration of my mother changed. I saw her as critical and moralistic. As a teenager I decided, "What she doesn't know about me she can not pass judgment on." So I kept much of my life very private.

Although she was a progressive on the political scene—giving her time to the Margaret Sanger/Planned Parenthood movement—I didn't find her views of my behavior very liberal.

However, since she was also a very caring parent there was little of an obvious nature I could rebel against. My way of breaking loose was to be self-contained and non-revealing.

I left for college at age fifteen turning sixteen so the years of my coming to full womanhood were on my own. On several visits home, when I was in torment about my life, I asked to talk to my father, alone. I knew that he would let me come to my own decisions whereas Mother would overwhelm me with her opinions.

During my married years she was there to help me before or after the births of our children. She was the major connector of family, the one who initiated letters and phone calls to my brother's family and ours, relating the Rogers' news. She remembered birthdays and Christmas in thoughtful ways and was interested in our various adventures. She wrote letters telling of my father's new interests and jobs. I replied in the same vein. Her letters were to my husband and me as though we were one and the same person. (My brother-in-law and his wife used to write to us combining our names into one word. Husband and wife had merged into one person.)

I believe mother was particularly proud to report to her friends the news of our happy marriage. Since I was following in her footsteps—being a good mother, housekeeper, decorator, hostess, and wife—her pride and love was constant. So it is no wonder that when I began to lose my sense of self in marriage I was afraid that I would be a tremendous disappointment to her and would lose her love. It took a long time for me to build up enough courage to reveal my agony to her and thus to my father as well, because they held no secrets from each other in regard to us). Although she was bewildered, sad, and disappointed in my break-up, she remained supportive to me through my troubled years.

More recently, as an adult with self-esteem intact, I have been able to share myself with her more fully. I know that I will do what I want with or without her approval.

I also see that I have taken on many of her good qualities. I am a nurturing, outgoing person largely because of the example she set. I have appreciated being a mother myself because she enjoyed her relationship with me when I was a child.

Suddenly, I find myself churning inside like a troubled sea. The vacation with my daughters is over. I've been lying in bed every morning for an hour pondering my relationship with my mother. I read what I have written, and it is all true. Yet it is void of the passion with which I feel it. I wonder if I dare write the letter which is deep inside me; wonder what tears and anger it will stir up. Is it fair to put on paper and possibly in print something I have not delivered to her person-

ally? Shall I protect her (and me)? I decide to write and later se
if it is appropriate to share.

Dear Mother,   January, 197
I look into the mirror—into my body and my heart, m
soul, and I see the *you in me*. I am writing this letter to try to sor
out which is really you. And which is the part of you I hav
incorporated into myself. Who am I? The acceptance I have o
you now is real. The poem—I meant it.

However, there is a context for that acceptance that ha
not been clearly stated by me, directly to you. It is the ange
and pain—yours or mine, or the you in me, about which I hav
not been direct.

I see you as having lost much of the identity you had as
younger woman. I see you as having given up your interest
and needs to create an environment of support for you
husband's career and his fame. That has angered and fright
ened me because I played that game for a long time mysel
Almost too late, I saw the you in me.

I see you as "doing for others" in order to avoid facin
yourself directly and asking "Who am I? What do I want out o
my life?" That a/void/dance is truly a dance into the void. It is
copout! It is an unwillingness to fight for yourself! Have yo
lost yourself?

And as I write that, I realize I am writing about me. M
submission into my husband's career was, in part, to cop ou
of not risking myself in the real world. Rather than say, "I'n
intelligent, I'm capable, I am creative and want to engag
myself in the struggles of the world," I let him do battle for m
and talked about his achievements.

Mother, I see you as having held in your resentments an
angers for years! Perhaps you didn't know what they were. O
perhaps you are afraid you will not be loved if you show you
anger. Or you may never have seen people get angry, mak
up, and become more intimate because of it. And I am angry a
you for not showing me the way.

And as I read those words, I am talking about me, as wel
I was not aware of my resentments in my marriage so I didn'
know how to let them be known.

Dear Mother, I see those resentments oozing into you
sore joints, your aching body. The scars on your milky whit
torso, the swelling of your joints, the bone marrow that won'

manufacture red cells, I *experience* this physical part of you—your body—as rage at the world. I am sensing your pain as repressed rage.

And when I read that sentence I say to myself, "You presumptuous daughter! Who the hell do you think you are, interpreting her physical pain as emotional repression?"

Then fear strikes me that I may age physically in the same manner and have to eat my thoughts. Tears come to my throat, and I don't know whether to cry or pound. Pounding is harder for me, as it is for you. And I need to pound!

Again I see the parts of you that I have incorporated—the you in me. I know I have repressed much anger also and I want to shout out! For you, for me, for women.

Speaking of anger, I have been angry at you for not allowing me to be angry at you. You seem to create an environment around you which says, "Thou shalt not get angry at me!" I have allowed that to control me. I was afraid you wouldn't love me if I got angry at you.

Reading that I realize how much of my own power I throw away when I say *you* don't allow me to get angry. At a deeper level it was my choice not to get angry at you.

As I criticize you for the peace-at-any-cost atmosphere you create, I look at what I do, myself. I know that I frequently give off the same non-verbal message. My daughters get angry at me, at times, but how much do I create the same environment? In the encounter groups I facilitate, people have difficulty expressing their anger at me. I know it is because I seldom express anger at any of them. So again, I see part of you in me.

Mother, I am disappointed that you did not make a claim for yourself and your interests when your children left home! You continually put your husband's profession first. Between age forty and sixty you missed an opportunity to become more fully you—more independent in your art work or fully effective with Planned Parenthood. Oh, I know that you used your talents and abilities at hobbies or as a volunteer, but you valued those creative times and yourself, as *second*-best. And that makes me sad. I believe you are worth putting yourself first.

As I reread that paragraph I realize how, when I went back to school to get my Master's degree and during my years as a psychological trainee, I placed my own work as an avocation. My children and husband were my vocation. Perhaps a that time an avocation was what I needed. But I could hav valued myself more in the process. As I remember this feeling I soften toward you and how you lived.

Mother, I see you as not knowing who you are when you are not needed by your children, your husband, or friends When I need you to take care of me, you rise to the occasion and feel good. When I (or others) don't "need" you, you seen to slump. It makes me feel as though you only love me or can feel good yourself when I am down. I don't like that. It als makes me sad. And scared—maybe I'll be that way, too.

I live my life, in part, to change the karma of the *you in me* In writing this, I find the anger and suffering in you and the anger and suffering of *woman*. I find the love and strength in me is the love and strength in you and womankind.

In writing this I am finding a deep bond and a determine purpose. Now is the time for me (and you) to go back an reread the poem I wrote to you and your answer to me. The meaning and purpose of it becomes more sharply focused. It in *context*.

As I look into our connection, I am looking into the mirror I see me, I see you. I am, and probably always will be, in the process of differentiating myself from you.

And what is the point of all this? I am discovering that the most important woman in my life is *You*, my mother. (I didn expect this at all when I started to write.) As I become aware my unspoken anger at you, I discover my anger at myself, an my own life becomes more focused. As I push against m image of you, I find my goals.

I want a strong identity of my own, with or without a husban or partner.

I want my own private work/studio room: a place to be b myself, undisturbed.

I want my own career, my own income, my own indeper dence no matter how interdependent I may become with partner, colleagues, or friends.

I want to know who I am when I am not needed by m

children, partner, or my friends. What is it that I am living for, within *me*? A forever question!

I want to be aware of my anger and learn how to express it constructively with the person involved.

I want to be a person with whom others can feel free to get angry. (I see this as closely connected to the previous point—if I know how to show my anger, others will find ways to reveal their anger at me.)

I want to understand the connections between my emotional state and any physical illness and learn ways, the best I can, to keep mind, body, and spirit united.

I want to love and appreciate my body and use it to express my sensual, sexual self: use it to dance my joy in life and to pound out the rage.

And so, dear Mother, in looking into the mirror of you/me I discover more of myself. (Only you can tell me which part of me is you.)

And when you are in the last process of dying, I would hope that I could hold you and care for you as you let yourself out of your body and into the beyond.

With love,

Natalie

I never showed that letter to my mother. Not only was he ill, which made such a confrontation inappropriate, but I ealized that the problems were my own.

As the year went on I learned to accept her more com-letely. I didn't have to agree with her to love her. Nor did I ave to do what she wanted to gain her love. (I hadn't ollowed her rules for a long time.)

It was my turn to mother her. As her body gave out there rere many women and men at her side daily—listening, ving, laughing, and cajoling. I traveled long distances to elp her through many physical crises. Many of us gained poignant insights as we watched her learn how to die. From total disbelief in any life after death she opened herself to the possibility of some other existence. Having seen reappearing white lights, and visions of family members already gone, she began the process of letting go.

As she lay in the hospital bed, I wrote what was to be my last letter to her.

Dearest Mom,   March, 197

My arms are around you as I write this, or tell this to you. Having talked to you two times this week on the phone believe I am hearing you wonder whether you want to struggle once more to stay in this world. As you lay in bed watching the sun set, with the peace of the horizon and the brilliant pinks in the sky, the world beyond may seem much more peaceful—and I am sure it is.

I cannot *know* but I see in you the extreme difficulty in letting go of this life to pass into some other form of existence.

Whatever you choose is truly all right, by me. I want you to know that you have given me *so* much love, nurturance and support in my life. Whenever you do die, I will miss you a great deal. But I also know that in me—your daughter—much of the loving spirit you have contributed will be carried on through me and all the other women daughters you have so generously given to.

Your life, love and spirit will always remain in our hearts.

If you should decide you would rather be in that other world I wonder if you realize you have some options in the hospital. You could, if *you* wish, ask for no more transfusions or IV's. You *could*, if you wish, ask to be at home with full nursing care—if you would prefer to die at home. I'm not sure whether you have considered these as options, because you are weak and our minds are not always clear when we are weak. But these are choices that anyone should have, with dignity of dying as one chooses.

If you decide to make the effort to regain some of your physical strength and be with us for awhile longer, that is a courageous and wonderful decision also. And I would help as that I can in your efforts. Again, please know how much I love and admire you. Whenever you go it will be a painful loss for

me. But I will always have the love and joy you have given me.
    Lovingly, your daughter . . .
P.S. I am asking Maria to read this to you. She is a real sister . . .

In the end, she gave me a gift of acceptance and love. As I was holding her hand she quietly slipped away. There was no groan, no motion . . .but I felt the life energy drain out of her hand, out of her arm, and lift up and out of her body, hovering in the room. I gazed at her face saying, "Mommy? Mommy?" And I knew she was gone.

It was shortly after her death that I had this dream:

> In my dream last night I was feeling very stressed because I was working on racial and women's issues. I was alone and fatigued. As I stood in front of a full length mirror putting on an earring, mother appeared to the left. I could see only half of her, the other half being hidden by the mirror. She had on the long white, stately gown she had worn to Grandma and Grandpa Rogers' fiftieth wedding anniversary. (I realize the significance of fifty since that is my age, now.) After some silence she looked at my depressed face and said very warmly, "Well, remember, *I* love you."

The next morning I felt Mother had really appeared, or so it seemed. Yet, it was at a mirror that I saw her, as though the Helen-part-of-me was giving me the support I needed to continue writing this book. Indeed, I pulled out the beginning of this chapter which had lain dormant for two years and found my title: "Mother and Me: A Look Into the Mirror."

The link between mother and daugher is special, of course. Women giving birth to, nursing, nurturing, watching their female children grow cannot help but see part of themselves in their daughters. As daughters having come from a womb while having one of our own, we have a special relationship to mothers.

My daughter, Frances, and I have co-led mother-daughter workshops. Frances has her B.A. in psychology and women's studies and is a strong feminist. Our main emphasis has been to open the channels of communication between adult daughters (sixteen and over) and their mothers. As write about my own mother many of the workshop statements come to mind.

Daughters frequently say, "Why aren't you a happier stronger woman so that I know how to live my life?" The mothers' answers are, "Look, young lady, life is no bed of roses, as you will find out. I *am* strong! You have seen me cope with all sorts of difficult situations. And I am as happy as I can be. I like my life—more or less—the way it is. Leave me alone. Go find out who you are and what you want, with my blessings. Stop asking *me* to be what you want for *yourself*."

When I understand that my mother did what she wanted in her life, as best she could with the resources she had and society as it was, I came face to face with "What is it I want for myself? Stop asking *her* to be what I want for *me*!"

Part Two
My Changing Attitudes
Toward Women

My attitudes toward women have changed dramatically over the course of my life. In the following pages I will explore how this came about.

My childhood chums were girls. Kithy, who lived down the street, was one of five daughters. Every day after school we played our imaginary games. As we rode our tricycles and later our bikes, we played dress up and took picnics down the lane. We each chose a role and played it faithfully for hours or even days.

"You be the mother, I'll be the father." Or, "Let's be teenage sisters." Or, "You be the Princess, I'll be the King." It was of no importance who was the male or female. We went to the jungles, reigned over slaves, explored the wild west or created ordinary family scenes. I don't remember quarrels, although there must have been some. We were "best friends," and competition, envy or arguments over who was to be in charge didn't arise. The give and take seemed fair. When boys entered into our games they were definitely temporary actors. We did not fight over their attention. Free in spirit, we used our bodies to run, swim, ride, jump, and dance.

In high school I also had a best friend. Ruth and I were both tall and athletic. In our small school we were frequently captains of opposing teams. The gym teacher saw to it we were separated to make the teams equal. We each played basketball, tennis, and field hockey. I am searching my memory for feelings of competition. I can't remember any. I *do* remember convincing each other of our worth and beauty. "You played a fabulous game!" Or, "I wish I had a figure as nice as yours." (Some envy, perhaps, but said in a way that did not put the other person down.) Our first boyfriends were also best friends so the four of us would sit in the corner drugstore eating chocolate sundaes with marshmallow sauce, flirting, and gossiping.

After returning to our separate homes, she and I would talk on the phone for hours. My mother said, "You two spend all day together, what on earth do you have to say to each other all evening?"

Who knows what we said? We were connecting—reassuring each other that "I am here for you!" As thirteen-year-olds we were helping each other along.

In 1944, when I was deciding on a college, a coed university would have been my first choice. One of my college expectations was to find a husband. Most young men were fighting the war at that time so coed campuses were three-quarters female. I chose a girls' school as a second-best option. My rationale went something like this: "Since most men are overseas, I would rather not be competing with other women for the few guys on campus."

It is apparent that at sixteen my concern was not only the quality of education but the opportunity to find "The Man." I was intuitively aware that this goal would set me against women, and I was worried I wouldn't stack up in competition. Better to drop out of the race entirely than come in last.

Looking back, I see that a women's college was a fortunate choice. In high school I had learned how to act less intelligent than I was in order to be attractive to the boys. At college I could let myself pursue my interests without fear. I found that women were bright, interesting, and fun. Our group of "stratoliners" (over 5'9") kept in touch by mail for fifteen years.

Then I transferred to a coed university and joined a sorority. The exclusive sorority-fraternity system was politically obnoxious to me, but I was told it was the only way to have dates or get invited to parties. My need to find a man was greater than my political ideals: I went through my "initiation" and became part of a system that excluded women who lidn't have the "proper" social background. I never forgave myself. I had fantasies of "exposing" the whole system hrough articles describing the "rush" process of eliminating he undesirables by one blackball vote. I didn't find these vomen to be the "sisters" they claimed to be in their lofty statements. As a sorority we attempted to be "number one" on campus at almost any cost. Old exams were filed away to help the students cram or cheat their way to the top. In sports and social standing the whole effort seemed to be aimed at being "the best." Such competition between sororities and between the women within the sororities diminished our ability to be intimate or give mutual support.

The formula seems apparent: enter men, women divide. As women we didn't know how to care for each other when our main motivation was attracting men and competing to be he number one sorority. There was a surface politeness and warmth between us, but one always knew that a female would drop her girl friend to be with a man. Or worse yet, "All is fair n love and war!" Translated as, "It doesn't matter what you do to your best woman friend in the effort to get your man."

It was during the mating game that I lost respect for women. More importantly, I lost respect for myself. My childhood acculturation had said, "Men are important people in he world. They are the thinkers, the doers; and you *need* one!" This led me to ignore and be ignored by my sorority sisters. Though I lived a year in that plush house, I can't remember any of their names.

As I left college, I entered courtship: a state of existence based on the assumption that "my man is primary, all others in my life are peripheral." At work my women co-workers were friends, but my male partner was my only confidant. Since I had my man engaged, women were no longer he potential enemy; but they were decidedly second n importance.

Marriage was a cocoon. I devoted myself to my husband, hen my children. I always had one or two close women friends with whom I discussed the children's development.

These relationships had their own special intimacy based on our concerns and hopes for our offspring. But we didn't know how, nor would we have thought it appropriate, to discuss the relationship problems we had with our spouses. And I thought discussions about world problems were beyond my scope. (An amazing switch; because, during my courtship days, I had been paid to travel through many states giving talks to high-school audiences promoting world government.)

I can remember how I ignored women, or considered them a second-best choice at faculty parties. If I could be the center of attention with four or five men around me, I considered myself a success. I captured these gentlemen by continually asking intelligent questions and letting them expound. Years later, a male friend confronted me directly when I did this to him. "Do you realize," he said, "that you never make any statements about what *you* think or what you do? You bait men with constant questions!" To him it was a bore—to be endlessly answering. For most men it was flattering and gave them the opportunity to parade their views.

I remember, in those married years, when a wife left town for some reason, we would invite the husband over for dinner. Many times husbands left town but I never invited their wives to be with us. I can think of many reasons—personal and societal—for such a double standard. My thoughts were, "I'd like to have another interesting, important man to talk with. Poor guy, he doesn't have his wife to feed him so I'll take him under my wing." Those were my own sexist attitudes.

As I was thinking about divorce, I had a "do it alone" attitude. Divorce was on the increase, but I only knew one woman who had gone through it. I didn't think of women as people to lean on, so I never asked her for advice.

One woman friend sought me out constantly, checking to see how I was. One day she heard the dead quality in my voice and didn't wait for me to ask for help. She got in the car, took me out for a ride (which I didn't want), talked to me so much I finally became angry at her. "Good, get angry with me!" she said, which made me even angrier. She jolted me out of my numbness as we spent the day wandering around Rockport by the ocean. It was the beginning of my recognition that friends take care of each other whether or not it is asked for. Fortunately (or unfortunately, depending on how you look at it), I was able to do the same for her a few months later when her husband told her abruptly on New Year's Eve that he was in love with someone else and wanted a divorce. She was numb and needed immediate support.

My women friends have often had this tendency—to wonder how a friend is getting along and check in by phone. Perhaps it is part of the mothering trait that out-of-sight is not out-of-mind. I've only had a few such men friends. Usually men and women call each other to make a date or get something accomplished.

It was after my divorce that I started to let women back into my life.

I heard the stories of second-class citizenship that my women clients told me. Their male therapists had advised them to "adjust" to their roles as housewives. At that same time the women's movement was saying, "Get out of the house." This forced me to look at some of my values. I believed it was more important for women to have a firm sense of a self and understand their options. That is, they need to be aware of who they are, what they want, and how to make good choices, whether that choice be to stay home or develop a career. The pendulum of my attitudes toward women was swinging back to appreciation, cooperation, and love after many years of mistrust, competition, and disinterest.

As a psychologist I was beginning to initiate groups and entitled the first one, "Training of Women Counselors of Women." My first confession as a group leader was, "I've never been in *any* women's group. I can help you learn counseling skills—you can help me learn how to share our female experience." On that first day I asked the women to take a roll of paper and draw pictures or symbols of their development as a woman. "Ask yourself, 'How did I feel as a young girl? As a teenager? As a young woman? Or middle-aged woman? What and who contributed to those feelings?' Include your feelings about being feminine, about your body image, about sexuality, assertiveness, and competence or any other feelings that arise in you."

Little did I know when I dreamt up this exercise the profound path of awareness that I would discover for *myself*! The mural I drew included me as a little girl in a sailboat with my father and brother. I came upon that important image of being "the crew" in life while the male captains charted the course.

Women as a Source of This Book

It was an unknowing woman client who sparked the first pages when she invited me to speak to the honorary society at her college ten years ago. To her, I must have been a model of success. But, my professional self image was still wobbly.

During that same year, a group of professors in the Humanities Department at MIT asked me to co-lead a five-day workshop. They wanted to increase their abilities to work as a team and to develop their person-centered teaching skills. The dozen or more teachers of writing and literature met in my playroom morning, noon, and night for a week. Patsy Cumming emerged as a friend with strength and perceptivity who would help me see myself as a writer. As an accomplished poet and co-founder of Alice James Books, she introduced me to the notion that women can create their own publishing firms.

I showed her the twelve pages I had written for my talk. It was the first time I had shared personal writing. Although I had completed a Masters Thesis, I had never sought the meaning of my *experiences* through writing. She let me know writing could be a *way* of thinking creatively rather than a product that displays the answers.

Those twelve pages ended with a description of my divorce. Friend and colleague Olivia Hoblitzelle urged me to describe what it was like after my divorce.

> I am dying for you to bring it up-to-date: that of being a gifted professional, single woman, therapist, and artist. What challenges has that brought? What are your new definitions of what it means to be a whole, free person? How about role expectations now?

Those questions fanned the flames. Her description didn't fit my self-image, however, so I asked her to interview me on those questions. We spent an afternoon sharing our perspectives on life in the present, which I tape-recorded. Again there were tears and rage as I uncovered more feelings about the struggle to be equal in an unequal world. She inspired me to further describe my life and learnings.

Olivia was trying to balance her life as mother, wife, therapist, writer; besides this she also needed to find time for meditation and spiritual growth. I know what a difficult balancing act that can be.

As I began to define myself as a professional woman, Jackie Doyle (then co-director of Greenhouse with Philip Slater and Morrie Schwartz) showed me that women do not have to be subsumed to their male colleagues. She was powerful, loving, and loved. And the men in the Greenhouse Training Program were trying to redefine themselves in relation to women and work—a refreshing experience.

Moving to California I reconnected with Lois Bateson. She and I had been colleagues at the University of Hawaii Counseling Center, where I had my first paid job. Her brilliance and radiance were not overshadowed by her well known husband. It seems significant that I would place my trust in a woman to guide me on my first hallucinogenic trip. She was the mother-bird on the Big Sur Gorda mountain, protecting me from a distance, never intruding but always available.

The impact of that experience was integrated at a workshop with another important woman in my life—art therapist Janie Rhyne. Competence and intellect are womanly attributes that ripen with age; I learned as I became her friend. With admiration I listened to her experiments in living, knowing I had similar options if I dared risk them.

She started me on my art journal—quick expressions of mood and feeling through color, line, and form. I painted my psychedelic trip with intense, vivid colors and flowing, symmetrical forms during her training program. (My hope is that someday this book can be published, with many of my pictures as illustrations of the exalted and low times of these past ten years. Friends who have seen the color picture version say it doubles the impact.)

Coeleen Kiebert lived for six weeks on her sailboat; it was parked in a harbor close to my Sausalito houseboat. She was spending concentrated time away from her family writing a lovely book on the creative process. We spent hours together critiquing each other's work. When I brought my art journals out of the closet, she encouraged me to use them as illustrations for my words. It never would have occurred to me. They were my private discoveries. I developed a slide presentation to go with my first chapter, "The Right to Be Me."

That slide talk led me to Latin America. After presenting it in Cuernavaca to a Latin American psychology audience, Jose Gomez del Campo translated it into Spanish and Juan LaFarga published it in his psychology journal. (Yes, some wonderful men have definitely helped and encouraged me along the way.) The Spanish version made me feminist friends in Chile, Argentina, and Nicaragua as I meandered through those countries during a six-month journey of "cutting loose" from old work patterns.

Dee Michener was one of the first women to confide in me about her relationship to her husband, about their troubles and, later, about her lovers. This opened me to tell, via letters (she had moved by then), some feelings about my first lover. I remember asking her to tear up the letters (to my regret,

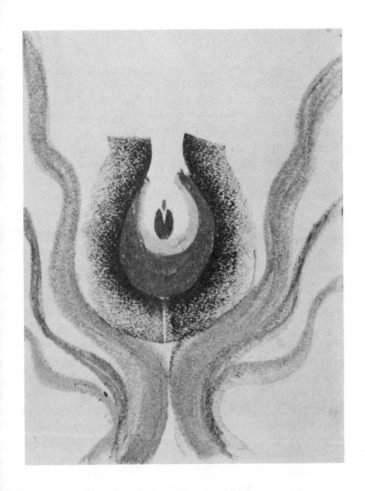

ow). To put in *writing* some of the pain I was having in my marriage and the delightful feelings of support and sexuality I was experiencing in a new relationship, terrified me. I never wanted anyone to know any of it! My sense of privacy in such matters was overwhelming. When, years later, she said, "Your next chapter should be about your lovers," I thought she was out of her mind. Yet she planted the seed for the idea which became Chapter Four. She has consistently given me impetus to finish this book, telling me her women friends and clients need and want it.

You may be wondering why I am spending time telling

about specific women (and men) who have encouraged and sustained this venture. "Put it in the preface," you say? No Women tend *not* to get the credit they deserve. They ar frequently the ideas behind the professor, the author, th senator, or even the President. But who says, "It was you ideas, your conversation with me, your suggestions tha helped shape this piece?" It is a woman's way—my way—t bring us all along, together. And the process of this boo seems as important to me as the product. The climb up th mountain is at least as important as reaching the summit.

My friendship with Adrienne Richard—author of fou novels and many short pieces—and her husband, Jim, ha persisted through long separations as we live on differen coasts. They both responded helpfully to this manuscript.

When Frances Vaughan and I met, we took an instan liking to each other. Knowing that friendship doesn't jus happen, we promised we would find the time to know eacl other. At that time, Transpersonal Psychology was a categor without meaning to me. She introduced me to the conceptua meanings of intuition, transcendence, and spirituality. Th fact that she completed her first book, *Awakening Intuition,* wa an inspiration for me to keep plugging away. When we spen an afternoon or evening together sharing dreams—dreams o the night and of the future—I come away revitalized. When began to back away from writing in a personal style (fearin; the exposure), she nudged me on—"Do it. It's important. It' your way of contributing to the world," she would say.

It was Leni Schwartz whom I called long distance a 6:00 a.m. as I awoke from my second terrifying nightmare c violent earthquakes. In my dream I was on the seventh floor c a dilapidated wooden building, lying in an old bed looking u; at the sky through the roof that had partially blown off. I wa overwhelmed with panic from the violent shaking. (In reality my lover of four years had just closed the door on ou relationship, replacing me with a dependent, clingin woman. And my mother was in the hospital, dying.) Leni voice came through loud and clear even though she wa barely opening her eyes: "I have some strong impressions, but what are your associations?"

"I don't know . . . I am terribly shaken!" I replied.

"It seems like a wonderful, positive dream," came her warm voice. "It is scary because it's about a monumental transition. The earthquake is shaking the foundations of your world. The protective roof has blown away. You are observing all of this from your bed, which is a safe place, a womb. And you are looking heavenward toward the sky—nothing but clear blue sky overhead. It seems like the next dimension as your journey moves into the spiritual realm. Also, being on the seventh floor could be a symbol of completion of a cycle."

Her words were reassuring.

Leni is creating a beautiful, fresh book about the psychological environment of pregnancy and birth. She combines her professional, artistic design talents with her love for people to create nurturing environments. Exciting people move into her sphere for intellectual discussions, and come away feeling replenished. She and I confess our self-doubts and buttress our special talents.

Maria Villas Bowen, a sensitive, intuitive therapist, is in tune with her telepathic, psychic abilities. I am learning from her that we all have that capability if we open ourselves. She was my stabilizing sister as we, and others, created a gentle environment where my mother could peacefully slip through the window of death.

Elizabeth Campbell, as executive director of the Association of Humanistic Psychology, is a woman leader I admire. She is forceful, warm, competent, and playful. She promotes the feminine principles in AHP and works to have equal representation. "You're wonderul," she hugs and assures me after I've vented anger and burst into tears confronting men I'm fond of who are not paying attention to male/female balance in our organization.

Lillie Leonard has read portions of this book (as has her husband, George) and given a helpful critique. She writes me

a delightful "you're nifty at fifty" poem. Also, she goes off fo
two months alone to dig into her own professional writing,
first for her.

Pat Ellsberg, an ethereal spirit with a clear-think
ing mind, leads us into deep meditation at some of ou
gatherings.

Char Horning, a bouyant, nurturing friend, is one of th
few midlife women I know who has remarried. One topic w
delve into as we picnic on a hillside is, "How can women b
married yet continue a "single" self image and identity?" She
like many of us, found a new identity and strength after he
divorce. In her new marriage she is learning how to maintair
that sense of self. It is all too easy to expect a husband t
protect, provide and fix things—at a cost to both partners.

The list of important women colleagues and supporter:
seems to grow as I write. Who would have believed that ter
years ago I thought men were more important than women
Some women push me further with feminist thought. The
have read more widely or are active in feminist centers
Maureen Miller, and Jeanne Adelman Mahoney have consis
tently challenged my feminist foundations, for which
am grateful.

I have mentioned several times in these pages the impor
tance of dance and movement in my life as I grow older. Ann
Halprin, another strong, creative woman who has turne
sixty, is a model of developing mind, body, and spirit
Immersing myself in her training programs for severa
seasons has led me to some new thoughts and experience
regarding creativity. As I integrate her work and that of Jani
Rhyne's art therapy with my own psychological training, I an
developing concepts and workshops around the creative con
nection: that is, movement puts us in touch with new feelings
which can be expressed through art, writing, music, or nev
forms of movement. We can dance what we paint or pain
what we dance or write a poem after moving and then put it t
music. One way to release the creativity within is to start wit
movement, where we are usually most inhibited. My work i

o create the inviting, safe environment in which we can explore in any media. Anna started me on this path.

For years, Rosemary Matson and her husband Howard have been behind me helping me push on. With Marie Wells, Rosemary, in her sixties, starts a new organization: Women in Transition. As a dedicated Unitarian, she is preaching about the centuries of heavy-handed male domination in religiou institutions.

Women who lead exciting, active lives in their seventie are a source of inspiration to me as I look toward such a futur for myself. My good friend Dorothea Stockwell started a com munity venture ten years ago at age sixty-three with he husband in Vermont. (I was thinking I was too old at fifty. N more.) She teaches, has a private practice, creates trainin programs, does her share of gardening and cooking, and trot off to folk dancing! Christine Sears Blaisdell, a medical docto turned therapist, has rebounded from being widowed twic and keeps such a lively pace she makes me feel like a turtle.

As I work in Latin America and Europe, I am moved b the response of women in these cultures. We reach out to eac other across language and ethnic differences.

I love these women. They love me. And that's how w will change this world: through love, determination, an mutual support.

We are intelligent, educated, middle-class (Americar women in midlife. We are "over the hill." That is, we hav worked hard as mother, as volunteer, as the power-behind the-throne, and as professionals. We are tired of inequality We have climbed that "hill." And now we are at the to looking over to our futures. We can see the lush fields, peopl harvesting the crops, a dark cave, rushing brooks, wild straw berries, and a snow-capped peak in the distance. Life i exciting if we understand ourselves and our society, drop ou fears and walk on through the valleys and forests keeping i touch. We have the ability and determination to put balanc into the society that has gone "tilt."

Women, today, are a revolutionary force. We are discov ering our self-worth, our personal strength and power. As u define new roles for ourselves—at home and in society—w will alter our world.

As men take time to discover their intuitive, nurturin feelings, and women find their competence and assertivenes: we—women and men—can work together to give ourselve equal opportunities: equal in all professions, in earning power, and in leadership (these three having been denied to most women); and equal opportunity for parenting, creating a nourishing environment for family, leisure, and long life (these being denied to most men).

As we find *internal* balance, there will be equilibrium between men and women. We will then also be able to open ourselves to more harmonious, loving relationships between *persons*.

ACKNOWLEDGMENTS

My women friends are given their proper place as the source and motivation of this book in the text of the last chapter. I also wish to acknowledge the love and support I have received from many men.

My father, Carl Rogers, has always been the earth from which my philosophical roots have been nourished. He values the integrity of each individual not only in his words but in his way of living. He has never dominated, controlled, or tried to push me. I have felt accepted and appreciated even when we disagree. When I suggested we create some workshops together, he was delighted. Working with him has always been the way I have come to know him and let myself be known. As a child, helping with a project was the way to our closeness. As an adult I have both admired and criticized him and his work. He has opened himself to understanding the problems of women, and I value his willingness to learn.

The men in the Greenhouse Training Program have had impact on my life. Philip Slater, Morrie Schwartz, Alan Nelson, Harrison Hoblitzelle, Lou Krodel, Paul Crowley, Charlie Derber and Jack Sawyer are searching for ways that women and men can better relate to each other and their environment. In my work with Alan I became more aware of how the personal is political. Philip, in his gentle way, pointed out how I perpetuated sex role behavior, myself.

Louis Krupnick was the first man to give me extensive feedback on my chapter, "The Right to Be Me!" I listened to his thoughtful, non-defensive reaction. It was encouraging to know some men are interested in getting out of the sex roles society has programmed for them. Since then, he and I have shared tenderness and tears, laughter and escapades.

It was Stephen Foster's personal intensity and enthusiasm for his work that enticed me out to the desert on my vision quest. He reads what I write, passes it on, and asks for more. We have an ardent caring for each other.

I feel in tune with John K. Wood and Jared Kass, both

staff members of our Person Centered Approach summer workshops. Although very different, each of these men is sensitive, soft, and competent. John and I know we can count on each other as we work. Jared and I push each other to create environments where movement, painting (including face painting), improvisations, music, and writing are the path to self-awareness and creative expression. When we are involved with our dance together, there is a lively connectedness. Both John and Jared encouraged me to get this book out.

These men, and others like them, are changing their values and living new roles. They don't have the need to be rich, powerful, or at the top. They *are* tops. We encourage each other to be whole people.

Finally, I want to thank the women who have helped me produce this book.

My decision to self-publish was made the day Freda Morris—a self-published author on self-hypnosis—offered to spend a day giving me expert how-to-do-it advice. When we tired of sitting, she offered to help spade my garden as we continued our dialogue. Zea Morvitz joined us that day with advice on book design.

Sarah Rush, my editor, spent many hours suggesting where I could expand the details of my story and where to clarify and condense. Her deft hand altered vague sentences into clean prose.

Zea Morvitz, my designer, used her artistic skills to pull the visual aspect of the book together with proper typeface, spacing, and picture arrangement, and then pasted up the galleys for the printer. She has given of herself all along the way.

Copy-editor Carolyn Means honed the fine details, looking for consistency, spelling and punctuation. We worked for nine hours, non-stop, around my dining table, making a deadline.

Judy Simmons has been a friendly, accurate typist and proofreader, eager to read each chapter.

These women have taken time from their major pursuits—Zea is an artist, Carolyn a potter, Sarah, now

psychology student—to assist me. They have cared about
the message I am putting forth as well as the form it takes.
It has been a meaningful, personal process of completing
these pages.

When looking for a typesetter I was delighted to find
scholar Michael Scriven and his Edgepress at the top of the
ridge in Inverness. His knowledge about self-publishing was
generously offered as his staff transformed the typewritten
page into attractive print.